HOME
BODY

HOME
BODY

a guide to creating spaces
you never want to leave

JOANNA GAINES

HARPER
DESIGN

An Imprint of HarperCollins Publishers

also by joanna gaines

THE MAGNOLIA STORY
MAGNOLIA TABLE

HOMEBODY

HarperCollins books may be purchased for educational, business, or sales promotional use. For information please email the Special Markets Department at SPsales@harpercollins.com.

Published in 2018 by
Harper Design
An Imprint of HarperCollins*Publishers*
195 Broadway
New York, NY 10007
Tel: (212) 207-7000
Fax: (855) 746-6023
harperdesign@harpercollins.com
www.hc.com

Distributed throughout the world by
HarperCollins Publishers
195 Broadway
New York, NY 10007

ISBN: 978-0-06-289668-1 (Magnolia special edition)
ISBN: 978-0-06-290982-4 (Magnolia signed edition)
ISBN: 978-0-06-288726-9 (Target Exclusive)

Library of Congress Control Number: 2018948770

Jacket design: Kelsie Monsen and Cassie Robison
Jacket front photography: Cody Ulrich
Jacket back photography: Mike Davello

Printed in the United States

First Printing, 2018

Quad

To my favorite people on Earth:
Chip, Drake, Ella Rose, Duke,
Emmie Kay, and Crew.

Thank you for teaching me that there
are far more beautiful things
than a perfectly kept house. You've
taught me what home truly means.

I'm a homebody because of you.

CONTENTS

INTRODUCTION

For nearly twenty years, I have been unknowingly writing this book in the back of my mind. Somewhere in my subconscious I've been filing away every design failure and every win. Going to school to learn this profession could have been quicker and less painful, but the upside to learning it the hard way is that these lessons won't ever be just ideas on a page to me. Every hard-won piece of knowledge feels like gold because I remember what that lesson cost. It's made me infinitely more passionate about this work that I get to do every day, and I hope I can communicate that same level of passion and purpose to you in this book. What you hold in your hands is the culmination of all that I've learned through the hundreds of homes I've designed over the years.

When I was deciding what I wanted this book to be about, there was discussion about filling its pages with beautiful, aspirational images, and I knew right away that that wasn't what I wanted. In fact, there's nothing I want less than for you to look wistfully at other people's "perfect" homes and feel defeated or wish that they were yours. From the beginning, I wanted this book to be a practical and useful guide that would empower and motivate you to create a home that communicates the soul and substance of the people who live within its walls.

I'm a homebody. There's really no other way to say it. The world can feel overwhelming with its pace and noise, its chaos and expectations. Home for me is like the eye of a hurricane. There's a certain calm I experience there no matter what is swirling about on the outside. Home is where I feel safe, it's the place where I am most known and most loved. If you were to ask my family, I'm pretty sure they would tell you the same thing about themselves: there is nowhere they would rather be than home. I think it's because our story is all around us there. When you walk in, you begin to see and experience the journey of us. Our home is layered with family photos, artwork, and objects that weren't chosen simply to make a design statement, but rather to tell the story of who lives there. I believe that what we surround ourselves with—the colors, the materials, the things—can be random and meaningless or they can convey some of the most important truths if we let them.

Throughout this book, you'll notice a theme of "telling your story" within your home. What I mean is that I want you to approach the design of your home with intention, to surround yourself with items that mean something to you, and choose furnishings and details that make you happy or inspired or contented. There is a certain skill all of us can hone, which is seeing the everyday items that we already own with fresh eyes. Look again at the unique pieces that you've collected over the years. Is there a story or memory associated with any of them? Maybe you find yourself drawn to the simplicity and clean lines of a modern chair or a hand-thrown vase from a favorite potter. Small details resonate with us for a reason, and I encourage you not to ignore them. They are how I learned to create a home that I genuinely loved. One that looked and felt distinct from any other because it looked and felt like us. We surrounded ourselves with meaningful pieces, mementos, and gathered treasures—some family heirlooms that point to our history, some flea-market finds that we couldn't leave without—all equally lovely to us.

I've come to realize that it's not uncommon for people to feel immobilized when they try to make their home a place that feels significant and unique to them. We can get so bogged down with design rules and comparisons that we forget to focus on the simplicity of choosing things that we love for our homes. It's not about sticking to a specific, prescribed style. *It's about story.* And the moment you make that subtle mind-set shift, all of a sudden you're set into motion. It becomes fun, freeing even. If nothing else, the one thing that I really want you to take away from this book is this: Rather than following arbitrary guidelines, try to focus on incorporating the things that matter to you and the people who share your home.

Sure, some people may have a knack for decorating and design, but here's the thing: it's not rocket science. Just like in all of life, you try and fail and then try again, and eventually you figure out what works for you. So allow yourself the freedom to mess up, whatever that means, or simply change your mind. Go ahead and paint the room a color other than beige.

Even if you decide you were *too* bold and you don't actually love how it looks, you can repaint it later. It is not the end of the world. You tried, you risked, you learned—and hopefully you had fun with it. Buy the rug you've been eyeing and see how it fits. If it doesn't work, return it. Rearrange your furniture. Twice. Or three times. Don't worry about it being perfect the first time. In fact, never stop rearranging. It helps keep your home alive and evolving. Let's not take ourselves so seriously. There's enough truly hard stuff in life, and creating your home should not be one of them. I believe that intentionality with a dose of creativity goes much further than money and flawless taste when it comes to making a house a home.

My hope is that wherever you are, you find a way to love the home you're in. Create a space where everyone who lives there feels at home. Again, more than anything, I hope that when you put this book down you feel encouraged and emboldened to thoughtfully design a home that tells a story without regard for perfection. It's a story worth telling because it's yours. That is how you create spaces you'll never want to leave.

Cheering you on,

Joanna

HOMEBODY 101: HOW TO USE THIS BOOK

DESIGN GUIDE

SETTLE IN

01

First things first: Light a candle, pour yourself a cup of coffee or a fresh iced drink, and get comfortable. Consider this book your tool, or somewhat of a companion, here to guide you toward a better understanding of how to create rooms that look and feel like you. This is how you begin to create spaces that you love to be in.

FRAME OF MIND

02

This part is really important: As you go through this book, remember that your home should be a reflection of you. It's essential to understand that it isn't about arbitrary design rules or guidelines, but rather owning your story and loving the home you're in today. Then you can begin to see that there's no point in comparing what you have (or don't have) with others. Every word, takeaway, and photo in this book is meant to cheer you on toward creating spaces where you love to be, whether you live in a rented apartment or your first (or third) owned home. It really isn't about a some-day dream house, it's about today. No matter the size or shape of the place where you live, it is worthy of gratitude because it's home and it's yours.

LEARN TO IDENTIFY

03

In the first chapter, you'll find a breakdown of six core design styles. I consider these to be the foundational genres that help make up your personal style. By being aware of which ones resonate with you, you'll begin to define and navigate your preferences. Throughout the book, you will find a unique mix of homes that I've designed as well as a few that were designed by others. Each of these homes represents a particular style profile that blends two or more of the core genres I've outlined to show how personal styles are iterated in different people's spaces.

THINK CRITICALLY

At the beginning of each chapter, I've proposed specific design components for you to consider as you make your way through each room. As you assess the spaces, do so with a critical eye, studying the styles and details that you see. Thinking critically is not about being critical. Rather, it's with thoughtful consideration that you can begin to identify the things you're drawn to and find yourself resisting. This approach will help you take stock of the design choices that really resonate with you.

TAKE NOTES

At the back of the book are pages set aside for note-taking, intended for you to use as you make your way through each chapter. Any time something resonates with you, write it down. Take note of things you like as well as those things that you dislike—both are equally informing. This is also where I hope you'll begin to dream up ideas for the rooms in your own home.

TROUBLESHOOT

At the end of each chapter you'll find a section that offers practical solutions for the most common pain points we experience in our homes, such as low lighting, small spaces, and outdated elements. I suggest a few examples for how you can troubleshoot these potential problem areas. Sometimes all it takes is a small mind-set shift or some creative reimagining to solve the design challenges in your home.

USE THE GUIDE

My hope is that by the end of this book, you've gained the confidence you need to translate what you've learned into the design of your own home. The design template at the very back will help, with sections designated for sketching a floor plan, troubleshooting, calls to action, where to eliminate, and where to invest. Tear it out when you're ready to start planning for the spaces in your home. If you need more room to dream, you can print additional templates at magnolia.com/homebody. Now it's time to get started. You've got this!

Roy Grady

1900 To set screw B.tongue
April 11 " W. bolt 106, 6/25th sh
May 31 " Cash 500 (89) 16th Mdse
Octo 8 " " 2810 Mc Farlau
Nov 3 " Bridles 250 (20) 14
" 9 " By Cotton 5000 (478)
Dec " " Brot from book
To Transfer to

1901
Jany

1.00
1.00
3.25
1.50

50

01

IDENTIFYING YOUR DESIGN STYLE

THE STYLES | Style can be interpreted in so many ways. Each of us has a clothing style, a hairstyle, a style of mannerisms and habits that are unlike anyone else's. Our preferences are the lens we look through to determine the things we like or dislike. Even if we can't always identify them concretely or put them into words, they're there, informing our daily choices. In this chapter, I break down a different kind of style, but one I believe truly matters. It's defined by how we feel when we enter a room—the things we notice, feel drawn to, or even find ourselves resisting. These subtle prompts help to inform our own personal design bent. And once we understand what that is, we can work to create a home that is not only inviting but feels meaningful to us as well.

In this chapter, I want you to get to know the characteristics and qualities of the six foundational styles I'm featuring in this book. As you find yourself responding to a certain look of a room, this will help you put language to what it is that you're seeing and feeling. This is by no means an exhaustive list—I'm unpacking these genres using generalizations and terms that may not fully define your style. Still, I do think

they will serve as helpful guardrails as you work to define a look that is all your own.

My hope is that what you discover about your preferred aesthetic will enable you to better define how you want to approach the design of every part of your home. What you will take away is a foundation, a combination of styles, or even simply a list of words that you've seen used here to describe something that speaks to you.

THE HOMES | I believe that visual examples are helpful when it comes to identifying your preferred design approach. Following the six foundational styles are twenty-two homes that represent a range and combination of those looks. I've given a descriptive name to each house and identified the primary styles it represents. Very few, if any, of these houses will be just one look or genre. They tend to be more eclectic than that. Every space you see in this book will reflect that notion because I believe that a gathered approach is essential to creating spaces that are a true representation of you and the people who share your home.

FARMHOUSE

[farmhouse] : the main dwelling place on a farm.

Historically, farmhouses were primary residences in rural or agricultural settings that were often passed down generationally. If you are drawn to a farmhouse style, you appreciate items that are homemade and authentic. Like the traditionalist, you appreciate the story behind a piece. However, you don't want it to feel ostentatious but rather grounded and humble. Instead of choosing pieces with embellishment and added detail, you prefer the inherent texture of aged materials.

KEY DESCRIPTORS

NOSTALGIC	COTTAGE	DISTRESSED
CASUAL	AUTHENTIC	EXPOSED BRICK
PRIMITIVE	INVITING	SHIPLAP
ORGANIC	AGED	WIDE PLANKS
GATHERED	SIMPLE LINES	PORCHES

MODERN

[mod-ern] : of or relating to present and recent time; not antiquated or obsolete.

The modernist prefers a minimal look. You are contented when a space is pared down to the essentials. You prefer clean lines in your furniture, cabinets, and light fixtures. The modernist warms up a space with texture and textiles, but isn't afraid of abstraction. For you, the beauty is in the simplicity of your space. Everyday items that are displayed are practical, not excessive. The modernist isn't as interested in story or sentiment. Instead, the comforts you surround yourself with tend to be more focused on form and function.

KEY DESCRIPTORS

MIDCENTURY	MONOCHROMATIC	ANGULAR
CONTEMPORARY	EDITED	ARTISTIC
RETRO	STRAIGHTFORWARD	AVANT-GARDE
OPEN CONCEPT	STARK	MINIMAL
SCANDINAVIAN	HIGH CONTRAST	TEXTURED

RUSTIC

[rus·tic] : relating to the countryside, rural; constructed or made in a plain and simple fashion.

This style takes its cues from nature. A rustic approach involves a lot of the same principles as farmhouse, with a particular focus on texture and materials. This style makes a statement, but not necessarily with color or embellishment. Instead, it is more about textures and organic elements, like raw wood beams, natural stone accents, and authentic hardwoods.

KEY DESCRIPTORS

RANCH	UNPOLISHED	ROUGH-HEWN BEAMS
SOUTHWESTERN	PATINA	NATURAL STONE
MEDITERRANEAN	TEXTURED	AGED COPPER
CABIN	DISTRESSED	TERRA COTTA
RAW	STUCCO	HAND-FORGED IRON

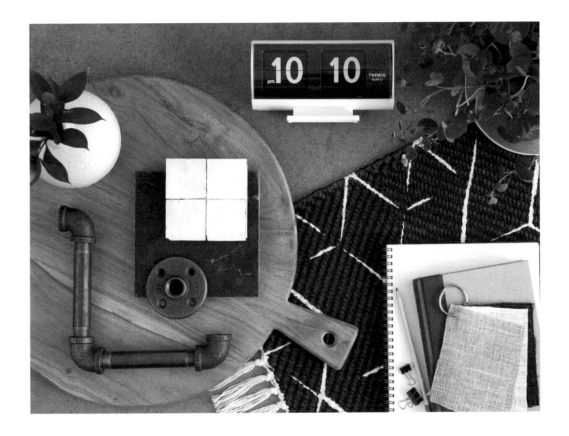

INDUSTRIAL

[in·dus·tri·al] : relating to or characterized by industry.

This style shares the fundamentals of rustic, but within an urban environment. You appreciate materials in their raw, unfinished form. However, instead of the rough-hewn beams and stone walls commonly associated with a more rural setting, this style is emphasized with elements like exposed ductwork and concrete floors. Inherent to this style is a focus on efficiency and multiuse. The industrialist is typically innovative in thinking and will repurpose items to serve new functions.

KEY DESCRIPTORS

LOFT	OPEN CONCEPT	METAL
URBAN	UTILITARIAN	GRAYSCALE
CONTEMPORARY	INVENTIVE	REINFORCED
MINIMAL	REPURPOSED	CONCRETE
FUNCTIONAL	UNREFINED	EXPOSED DETAILS

TRADITIONAL

[tra·di·tion·al] : habitually done, used, or found; long-established.

The traditionalist is attracted to historic details and classic shapes. When it comes to a piece of furniture, you appreciate seeing traces of adornment and embellishment. When you walk into a room, you want to know the story behind the time-honored pieces you see. Architectural elements, such as heavy trimwork, paneled doors, and built-in cabinetry are hallmarks. If this is predominantly your style, you are likely to approach the design of your home using tried-and-true techniques rather than attempting to push the envelope or try the unexpected.

KEY DESCRIPTORS

CLASSIC	STATELY	CRAFTSMANSHIP
EUROPEAN	ANTIQUE	BRASS ACCENTS
HISTORIC	STORIED	ORNATE TRIMWORK
TIMELESS	REFINED	FIGURATIVE ART
SOPHISTICATED	POLISHED	WARM WOOD TONES

BOHO

[bo·ho] : having an informal and unconventional mix of elements and motifs.

Boho style focuses on objects with a story that are rich with character and detail, but expressed in a more casual, free-form way than the traditionalist. This style doesn't rely on historical standards. Rather, it strives to be vibrant, irreverent, and quirky. If you identify with this look, you aim to chart your own course and are typically drawn to rich colors, bold textures, and mismatched patterns. You don't mind organized clutter. Rather, layers and collections are indicators of a well-loved home.

KEY DESCRIPTORS

VINTAGE	TRAVELED	PATTERNED
ECLECTIC	TEXTURED	WOVEN TEXTILES
LAYERED	COLLECTED	UNIQUE SHAPES
WHIMSICAL	PLAYFUL	EXOTIC PLANTS
COLORFUL	UNCONVENTIONAL	QUIRKY DETAILS

Our Farmhouse
NAME

Intentionally designed around how my family lives and interacts, I gave the interior of our farmhouse a consistent color palette and added personality by layering in meaningful pieces. I chose to contrast the white, weathered walls that show up in nearly every room with strong black metal accents. The inherent character of this old house is highlighted in the simplicity of our furnishings and decor.

STYLE FORMULA

farmhouse	████████████
industrial	███

The Reimagined Retreat
NAME

Formerly a neglected barn, this home reflects farmhouse elements that are original to the property, with modern updates that make it clean and practical. Ample natural light keeps the space from feeling dark, making this an ideal rural retreat.

STYLE FORMULA

farmhouse	████████
industrial	████
modern	██

The Elevated Ranch

NAME

This quintessential ranch home has been constructed using rustic materials that reflect its surroundings. Traditional furnishings have been thoughtfully incorporated to elevate an otherwise rugged space.

STYLE FORMULA

rustic

traditional

The Humble Abode

NAME

The soft gray color palette, decorative trimwork, and classic light fixtures throughout this house establish it in a traditional style. Accents, such as distressed wall decor and ticking-stripe upholstery, also give a nod to a classic farmhouse style.

STYLE FORMULA

traditional

farmhouse

The Refined Monochromatic
NAME

Unique objects and unexpected patterns make a statement in this home. Every piece on display feels like a work of art, and nods to both traditional and modern aesthetics.

STYLE FORMULA

traditional	████████████
modern	█████████
boho	██

The Charming Manor
NAME

Much of the original architecture of this historic home has been left intact and any new details the homeowner has added are either vintage or personal, creating a layered depth of story in every room.

STYLE FORMULA

traditional	████████████
boho	████

The Uptown Industrial
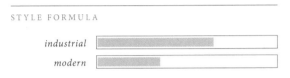

NAME

Exposed ceilings, warehouse-style windows, and stainless-steel accents define this industrial loft, while warm wood wall paneling brings in a soft, modern element. A sophisticated use of color adds an unexpected twist.

STYLE FORMULA

industrial

modern

The Colorful Industrial
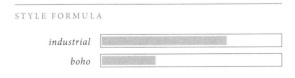

NAME

The exposed steel framing and raw architectural elements define this house in an industrial style, which is balanced by rich color choices and an eclectic collection of furniture.

STYLE FORMULA

industrial

boho

The Homespun Cottage

NAME

This 1740s farmhouse is steeped in history and character. A mostly neutral color palette and occasional modern pieces offset the aged architecture for an approach that feels warm, interesting, and practical.

STYLE FORMULA

farmhouse
traditional
modern

The Eclectic Farmhouse

NAME

The structure of this 100-year-old farmhouse is rich with original detail. A modern, Moroccan style is incorporated in the form of jewel-toned textiles and distinct patterns for a unique combination of charm and authenticity.

STYLE FORMULA

farmhouse
boho
modern

The Layered Bungalow
NAME

The original Craftsman architecture of this house has been preserved and blended with modern details. Boho textiles are used throughout to suit the home-owner's eclectic style.

STYLE FORMULA

farmhouse

modern

boho

The Tailored Tudor
NAME

The original cottagelike character of this home is brought back to life with simple traditional updates. The tailored look of the home's exterior is supported by the architectural details inside.

STYLE FORMULA

traditional

The Sophisticated Modern
NAME

Boasting all of the architectural hallmarks of a midcentury house, this residence has been updated with sophisticated finishes, including black cabinets, gold hardware, and sleek marble counters.

STYLE FORMULA

modern	▓▓▓▓▓▓▓▓▓▓▓
boho	▓▓

The Minimalist Lodge
NAME

Saltillo flooring spans the length of the entire house, making a strong, rustic statement. The southwestern vibe is met with asymmetrical architecture and other modern elements, including a concrete-slab entryway bench and open shelving.

STYLE FORMULA

modern	▓▓▓▓▓
rustic	▓▓▓▓▓

The Rustic Minimalist

NAME

Built with a small footprint, every corner of this home is maximized using well-purposed and low-profile furnishings. The rustic style of the threshing-floor wood planks and raw-edge furniture offsets the loftlike industrial architecture.

STYLE FORMULA

industrial	
rustic	
modern	

The Vintage Dwelling

NAME

Furnished with classic midcentury modern pieces, this home also incorporates bohemian and southwestern elements in the form of retro-patterned wallpaper, fiber macramé plant hangers, and a stucco wall texture, embodying the quintessential boho style.

STYLE FORMULA

modern	
boho	

The Unexpected Estate
NAME

The sophisticated and formal architecture of this home is balanced with an interior that is defined by whimsical elements and modern detailing throughout the interior.

STYLE FORMULA

traditional

modern

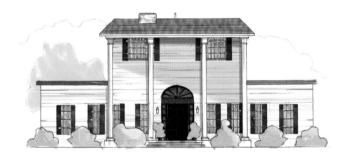

The Stately Traditional
NAME

This historic estate maintains much of its original architecture. It has been renovated to reflect its sophisticated traditional style, while still making room for a few modern and rustic statements.

STYLE FORMULA

traditional

modern

rustic

The Handcrafted Hideaway
NAME

The traditional decor and rustic details of this country home are balanced with simplified and modern counterparts.

STYLE FORMULA

traditional	
rustic	
farmhouse	

The Daring Elemental
NAME

Bold architectural choices are enhanced with colorful and iconic midcentury furnishings that help to soften the overall feel of this home. Cinder-block walls and stainless-steel accents add an industrial statement.

STYLE FORMULA

industrial	
modern	

The Timeless Chateau

NAME

The European aesthetic of this home's exterior is continued inside, with white oak hardwood flooring, decorative trimwork, and aged antique furniture. Distressed tiling in the entryway and sunroom contribute an old-world rustic texture.

STYLE FORMULA

traditional	
rustic	

The Restful Villa

NAME

Natural stucco, raw wood, and stone textures make a strong rustic statement in this ranch-style house. This look is balanced by clean-lined modern light fixtures and cabinetry alongside traditional decorative details.

STYLE FORMULA

rustic	▭▭▭▭
modern	▭▭▭▭
traditional	▭▭

ENTRYWAYS

My home is my safe place, it's my exhale. The way my family feels about home is of the utmost importance to me. It's an honor to get to create a place that we all genuinely *want* to spend our time in. One of the reasons I am so passionate about my work is because I deeply want this for everyone.

At our house, the front porch and entryway are our first warm welcome. There's this feeling that starts to unfold as soon as I pull into our driveway and see the rockers where we often watch the sunset on summer nights. Even the dirty old boot scraper the kids use nearly every day prompts me to smile as I cross over our welcome mat and in through the front door.

I don't know if other people get sentimental about seemingly random inanimate objects like I do, but I don't see them like that. I've always seen the story behind them.

I can feel myself begin to unwind as I shut the door behind me, surrounded by the glow of our entryway. This soft light feels to me like the best kind of welcome, the front door shutting like the best kind of hello. The world and its chaos, the day and its demands—all of it falls silent. *I am home.*

We tend to pour much of our design energy into the core areas of our homes, the places where we'll entertain or spend most of our time as a family—I get that.

And philosophically speaking, I do believe that what's on the inside matters most. It's a value I hold for myself, and that I teach to my children. But I've learned that tending to the outside has a pretty profound effect on how we feel on the inside.

The small, thoughtful details that are on your porch steps or by the entrance to your home, like the planters, sconces, or a welcome mat, can set the tone for the way your space welcomes you and your guests inside. The distinct details you put here should feel like you just as much as what you've created on the other side of your threshold.

These details communicate something to our guests, and even to strangers driving by, but perhaps even more important, they're communicating something to your own family. These first impressions are like a visual acknowledgment that we care about the space we come home to every day—inside and out. This is where everyone enters the house every day, so I think making that space—whatever shape it may take—feel important is valuable, and should be intentional.

Some front doors open to a classic entryway or foyer, but there are plenty of atypical spaces as well. In my house, what we have is a narrow hallway on the back side of the front door. It's not an ideal setup as the space is small and not fully defined, but we've outfitted it with things that are meaningful to our family, and we've made it a functional and inviting space. On our entryway table we keep a large antique Bible that I just love. This somehow establishes both this area of our home as well as who we are as a family.

Having worked on many different houses, I've seen entryways take on all kinds of forms. In some homes, you might walk straight into a wide-open gathering space. In others, a large wall greets you first. No matter what shape your space may take, sometimes all it needs is a console table or a unique piece of furniture and a coatrack or boot tray to help it function efficiently. These practical elements also help to keep essentials such as shoes, jackets, and backpacks from ending up scattered around the house.

I am a strong believer that functionality doesn't need to be sacrificed to make a space feel inviting. When we provide specific places for family members and guests to kick off their shoes and stash their keys or bags, it's a way of saying: *Come on in, we care about you, you're welcome here.* And something as simple as a lit candle can help these first moments communicate just that.

Entry spaces can often lack definition when their size and shape are awkward and difficult to design around. If a traditional entryway doesn't already exist in the house, the hard part can be knowing how to carve one out. Entryways are often a challenge. But there's a reason why it's the first room that we're featuring in this book. Choosing to make this part of your home count by filling it thoughtfully is how we can create a space that really does welcome whoever enters. The small details are what greet us at the door and invite us inside, whether we are home after a long day of work or from a trip to the grocery store. When we intentionally design a space with our needs and preferences in mind, we can feel known as soon as we walk in. And our visitors see that. They see who we are, what we need, what matters to us. No matter who it greets, our entryway should be a well-thought-out welcome.

Because this space serves as our first hello, we also want it to be beautiful. And that's because no matter where you live or how big your paycheck or your family is, your home can be a place that you love to return to and invite others into as well. Your entry should serve your lifestyle and tell of who you are and what you care about. This may sound overly ambitious, but I'm okay with that. This also may seem like a lot to accomplish in a relatively small space. But what I have learned in my own home and in the entryways I've designed over the years is that it's the everyday, thoughtful details that will distinguish a place as distinctly *yours*.

(*Page 32*) Most of the furnishings in our entryway at the farm are antiques I've collected over the years. The bench offers a place for our family and guests to comfortably put on or take off their shoes. The oversize mirror adds an ornate element and its reflection of the armoire on the opposing wall makes this long, narrow space appear larger. The herringbone brick pavers accentuate the farmhouse look, while the old hanging lanterns tie into the stair railing and add contrast to the neutral shades in this space. (*Page 34*) I think this antique armoire is as pretty as it is functional. Behind its doors is plenty of storage space. A unique black chair adds impact to this small entry and helps tie in the subtle black accents throughout the space. (*Above*) Since this area serves as the introduction to our home, I've made it welcoming by mixing practicality with visual interest. The antique gate, paired with tapered vases filled with greenery, complement the angled negative space of the stairs while the console table and papier-mâché bowls serve as catchalls.

CRITICAL
THINKING
IN DESIGN

ENTRYWAYS: WHAT TO CONSIDER

The entryway sets the tone for your entire home. Each one we're sharing in this chapter, though diverse in style, size, and aesthetic, illustrates how a bit of intention and effort can make this relatively small space the kind of warm welcome you want to share with your family and friends.

MAKE A STATEMENT

- Whether your house is large, tiny, or somewhere in between, your entry is likely to take up only a small portion of square footage. Take note of how these spaces are elevated with unique design choices, like interesting floors and statement-making light fixtures and furniture.

KEY FUNCTIONS

- This is essentially the spot where people drop things when they walk in the door, so pay attention to how functionality has been incorporated into these entryways.

- Identify the floor plans that are most like yours.

- Find the elements in each entryway that seem to be serving the homeowner's lifestyle both in function and personal style. These might include hooks, baskets, and catchalls, as well as sentimental pieces like art or a favorite antique. Consider how you might translate these choices into your own entryway.

THE ELEMENTS

- KEY HOOK
- SCENTED CANDLE
- CONSOLE TABLE
- LAMP OR SCONCES
- ACCENT CHAIR OR BENCH

- WELCOME MAT
- BOOT TRAY
- COATRACK OR HOOKS
- CATCHALL
- OVERSIZE MIRROR

This grand entrance at Hillcrest Estate called for more substantial furniture, like this round table and large bench. While it may not be typical to place a table right in the middle of an entryway, it helps define the entry so it doesn't fade away into the larger context of the room. The rug beneath the table offers a subtle texture to warm up the black-and-white color palette. The bright white walls, trim, and ceiling give this space a light and airy feel, and allow the furniture and art to be the focal point of the room. The oversize functional pieces, like the bench, coatrack, and umbrella holder invite any guest who enters to stay awhile, and architectural drawings of the house's original structure offer a sense of personal and historical significance. As a finishing detail, I like to incorporate fresh greenery whenever I can. In a larger space like this, a dramatic arrangement feels just right.

The front door is the focal point of this entryway. A glass door like this, bordered by additional sidelights, allows in plenty of natural light. That, coupled with an oversize mirror and light walls, makes for a bright, welcoming entry.

The first thing that strikes me about this entryway is the beautiful fiber art hung above a functional bench. It helps introduce the colorful aesthetic that this family loves and has used throughout their home. This particular entry is narrow, so I added an oversize mirror to make the space feel larger. It also brings a note of drama to this otherwise simple space. This approach works particularly well if you have a mudroom or secondary entrance that serves as the more hardworking space.

This entry is simple, but the elements have been purposefully chosen to make a statement about the owners' style. They wanted a rustic aesthetic throughout their home but also felt drawn to modern and southwestern details. What we've created here is a combination of these styles with a clean, modern concrete bench and Saltillo tile flooring. The baskets, plants, and pillows offer a nice welcome in this simply designed entryway. While baskets are a great solution for stashing everyday essentials, pillows offer a warm vibe, and plants help bring the space to life.

On one side of this entry (*left*) is a simple console table styled with candles and artwork. The light above it subtly highlights the framed art and lends indirect light to the space. Many people have a coat closet by the front door to conceal jackets and purses, but if you don't, consider adding a wall-hanging coatrack, like this one (*above*) where I attached simple hooks to this piece of antique architecture. To bridge these two sides of the entry, I chose a unique floor design, and because it was no more than an 8' x 10' area, it didn't break the budget to add some personality to this entryway.

The warm tones of this entryway are immediately inviting. There's not a lot of stuff taking up space in this entry, which lets visitors know that the pieces that are here—a chair, a single piece of art, a perfectly placed mirror, and a table styled simply with books and a welcoming bouquet of flowers—are important enough to the homeowners to serve as the first things guests see when they enter the house.

In this entryway, I wanted to incorporate a unique tile inlay that would add a bit of interest to this home. The tile, paired with the chair rail, adds to the definition of this space, making it feel more substantial and distinct from the rest of the house. The antique books displayed on the entryway table add aged details without it feeling too cluttered and overdone, maintaining the clean, minimal aesthetic the homeowners wanted. The antique console table and framed book pages offer a sense of story and established design to this newly renovated space.

TROUBLESHOOTING

DRAB DOORS

An old front door can really date a house. Update your entry with a new door or paint your existing door a color that better suits your style. Adding sidelights or a new door with a window can help transform a dark entry into a light-filled space.

LACKING INTEREST

If your area is separate, distinguish it with interesting flooring or tile. If you have an open floor plan, you can simply add a pretty rug or runner.

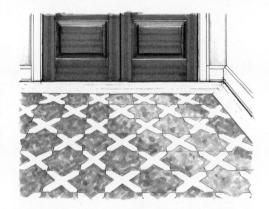

NOT ENOUGH STORAGE

Furniture can add purpose and utility to your entryway. A bench seat with storage space beneath, a chest of drawers, or baskets all make ideal solutions for hiding clutter. For a more lived-in look, a coat rack and wall hooks add important functionality.

NO DEFINITION

Layering in pieces like candlesticks, greenery, framed photos, or artwork can make the entry feel warm and inviting. If your space is enclosed with walls, wainscoting is a type of molding that can be applied to the lower half of each wall. This addition will create visual interest and help define the space.

POOR LIGHTING OR LOW CEILINGS

For low ceilings, you can install a flush mount or semiflush light fixture. These hang closer to the ceiling and typically have a low profile. If you have tall ceilings, a chandelier or hanging pendant will add light as well as visual interest to your entry. In a space with poor lighting, you can paint the walls and ceilings a light color or hang a mirror on the wall to make the space feel larger and brighter.

OUTDATED STAIRS

Updating your railing and stair material can make a huge impact. For worn-out or outdated carpeted stairs, rip it out altogether to install wood treads and risers, or consider a carpet runner (which looks like a long rug laid out over the stairs). You may want to stain the treads to match the wood flooring throughout your house and paint the risers to match the trim color. If you want to update the look of your railing, you can simply paint it. For a bigger statement, replace the railing altogether with updated spindles or iron railing.

03

LIVING ROOMS

Before we moved into the farmhouse, I used to treat my living room the same way I imagine a museum curator might handle an exhibition of treasured artifacts. I filled it with only the most beautiful pieces I could find, ones I was sure would look impressive to any guest who might stop by. I longed for it to look perfect around the clock, so I spent many hours a day tidying up couch pillows and immediately picking up any messes my children made, sometimes while they were still making them. And then one day, I looked around our living room that I had so carefully assembled and realized it didn't look anything like our family. Not one of us was represented in this space that was supposed to be central to us living life together. On top of that, I had spent so much of my time cleaning up any trace of my kids that this room had become a place they didn't even feel comfortable in. It was then that I realized I had let the pursuit of perfection inform how I designed this space instead of the people who were actually supposed to be enjoying life in it. This was a pivotal moment for me as a designer.

Because of this experience, the living room has become one of my favorite parts of the home to design for clients. I've made the mistake of reaching for a misguided ideal, and am now happy to help others avoid going down that same path themselves. It's an honor to be a part of creating something that really speaks to a family or an individual in a way that helps them live life more intentionally with the people they care about. Perfection never leads you there. I'm conscious of making sure they can actually see themselves *living* within the design of this space. Of all the rooms that fill a house, perhaps this is the one that should feel most like *home* to nearly everyone. It should be a soft spot in which to land after a long day. It should carry you through the ebb and flow of life's seasons, molding itself to support your needs. At the farm, it's where we can take a deep breath, relax, and settle in to catch up on one another's days. It's also where Chip takes some of his best Sunday afternoon naps. These are the moments that epitomize what home means to me, and they so often happen in the living room.

In many of our homes, this room will end up being multifunctional. On a daily basis it might serve as a resting place, but it's also where we entertain guests. This means it should be as welcoming to our family when they want to kick back and relax as it is to visiting friends. When it comes to furnishing a living room, it's natural to want to reach for the

prettiest sofa and tables you can find. But when you're investing in a core living space, something beautiful alone is not sufficient. It's equally important that the pieces you choose are also comfortable. So when I'm looking for furniture, I first think about what my family will actually want to sit on and where my guests can land when they inevitably start to wander toward a comfy seat to continue a good conversation. I love trying to reach this balance of creating a living room that is equally beautiful and livable.

Technically, our own living room isn't even a room at all, but more of an extrawide hallway that connects our entryway to our kitchen. Even though it's not your traditional square with at least three walls, when we moved in, it was the only option we had, so I worked with it. I started with the basics, knowing we'd need at least a sofa, a coffee table, and a chair. I placed these pieces in a way that would give the room some shape, and my family just settled in over time, even if it wasn't yet exactly the way I wanted it to look. We learned how to make the best of what we had and from there I slowly started to layer in the details. If I added a lamp or an end table it was because I had noticed a need for one arise; it was never just to fill up the space. I have a sincere love for fireplaces, but it just wasn't in the cards for this room, so instead I sought to create an unconventional focal point that was both beautiful and meaningful. Again, I didn't rush this just to fill the empty spot on the wall. It wasn't until sometime later that I came upon the large antique clock that was missing the hour and minute hands. It now hangs on the wall above our sofa, and to me, it symbolizes grace in our day-to-day life and that time at home is never wasted. I love how it helps to tell our story as you move from the entryway to the heart of our home.

I have grown really contented with our living room, as small and quirky as it might be, and I think it works perfectly for our family. Because of its unique footprint, it really forced me to take my time furnishing it. Every detail was hard-won and ended up getting layered in organically over time. Maybe

that's why I love it so much. It was through the process of creating this space that I really owned never being apologetic about furnishing a home slowly. In fact, it's become a bit of a design philosophy for me. I cannot encourage you enough to gradually add to your home one beloved piece at a time.

If you are wanting to give your living room a simple refresh, please don't take this to mean that you should toss out everything you currently own. This is more about scaling back to the things you can't live without in order to create some space for your real, beautiful life to unfold. If you have a piece of furniture that you like but it somehow falls a little flat, consider updating it with a fresh coat of paint or unique hardware. Sometimes just a simple tweak to your existing pieces can make all the difference. Other times, it might mean giving your eyes a chance to see the space as a clean slate by removing the items that cause clutter. I love adding character to a house wherever I can, but that is a different thing

entirely than what I'm talking about here. Filling a room with the things you think you should because you've seen someone else do it that way or because you just want it to feel finished will never yield a home you truly love. You can make a room feel both beautiful and complete without filling every corner and surface with a bunch of random stuff. Now, if your living room happens to be filled to the brim with pieces you absolutely love, keep enjoying them and don't let me get in your way! The point here is: Our homes should be a source of happiness to the people who live there, so surround yourself with things that you love and let go of the rest.

I am thankful that a room exists for the purpose of giving us a spot to rest and to gather with the people we love, even if what we have is not our ideal shape or dream setup. Instead, what we can create is a place where the stories and memories of our lives are sewn into its very fabric. And that should only get better with time.

(*Page 54*) I've always been drawn to the classic combination of black and white, so I wanted to make this the primary color palette throughout our home. The black accents of the textured rug, modern leather chair, and wall decor offer contrast to the white shiplap walls. (*Page 56*) Anything that I've chosen to hang on our walls is significant to our family. The antique street sign is from New York City, where Chip and I honeymooned. An antique safe acts as an accent table for design books and a plant. (*Above*) I wanted to place something purposeful and beautiful in this spot since it's a natural focal point when you walk into this main living area. We found this piano when we were doing a walkthrough in a potential remodel, and I loved it instantly. When we got it home and cleaned it up, we realized it had been painted this beautiful shade of green, which happens to be one of my favorite colors, and exactly the color addition this black-and-white space needed.

CRITICAL
THINKING
IN DESIGN

LIVING ROOMS: WHAT TO CONSIDER

Living rooms may be where you see the widest range of formality and purpose of any room in a home. Some people have multiple living spaces where they can dedicate an entire room to function, typically as a comfy landing spot for the family, and then another more formal space is set aside for special occasions. Others have an open-concept living area that they consider multioperational, much like we do. It's a place where our family can relax as well as where guests can settle in when we're entertaining. No matter what size and shape your living room may be, how this space is designed and styled conveys your priorities to anyone invited in.

HOW IT MAKES YOU FEEL

- Determine what the style and design of each of these spaces is communicating and what you want to be reflected in your own living room.

- Notice the details of the rooms in this chapter: pieces on the walls, the furnishings, storage, or bookshelves. Take note of what you are inspired by for your own living room.

CREATE SPACE

- Pay attention to furniture arrangements and seating solutions.

- If you like the pared-down look of some of these spaces, think through what you could stand to lose in your own living room.

THE ELEMENTS

- ACCENT FURNITURE
- CANDLES AND CANDLESTICKS
- WALL DECOR
- THROWS AND PILLOWS
- UNIQUE OR PERSONAL ARTWORK

- COMFORTABLE SEATING
- COFFEE TABLE
- LARGE AREA RUG
- GREENERY
- STORAGE BASKETS

I'm always drawn to well-restored spaces. The owners of this farmhouse have achieved a beautiful balance of old and new in this living area. The rich tones and dark accents make a strong statement all while creating a very comfortable environment. Although dark paint colors may feel intimidating, they can add an immediate dose of warmth. This room seems to emphasize that it doesn't matter what season it is outside, it will always remain warm and cozy within. There are a lot of details that command your attention in this room. I am immediately drawn to the hand-hewn beams, the bold color of the walls and trim, the beautiful wide-planked knotted floors, and the exposed brick of the fireplace. Together, these elements create a primitive, worn-in aesthetic in this living room.

Hillcrest Estate, a historic home built in the early 1900s, has a unique and grand way about it. When we decided to convert this beautiful property into a vacation rental in Waco, we wanted to keep as many of the original characteristics as we could. We also sought to give it the updates it needed to reflect an inviting, comfortable home away from home for our guests. The house's main living room is large, so in order to create definition, I placed an oversize coffee table in the middle of the rug. Then I positioned two flanking sofas and a chair on either side of the coffee table to help further define the sitting area in this wide-open room. The Chesterfield sofa adds a bit of formality and sophistication, which fits the charm of this historic home. To balance that look, I added my favorite design element in this room—the antique door built-ins. I wanted them to look as though they were built in with the house one hundred years ago rather than brand-new additions. I found this particular pair of vintage doors at a nearby antique show and they were just what I was hoping for. If you have existing built-ins or you're installing new ones and you like this look, search for antique architectural pieces that you can incorporate into the design. The mix of the old doors beside the new cabinet soften what could otherwise feel like a very formal room.

The main living area of this ranch house shares an open space with the kitchen and dining room, so I kept the look of the family room neutral to allow for a seamless flow. The antique mantel ties into the ceiling beams overhead for a unified look. The windows, doors, and built-ins were painted black to update the main room and make it feel more refined. Because this property sits on a ranch, I wanted to layer in subtle nods to its rustic surroundings, so I incorporated old-hewn beams and a stone surround on the fireplace, all of which mix well within the neutral palette of the walls and furnishings. The antique area rug adds a depth of color, which, along with the throw pillows, contributes to a cozy vibe.

The power of contrast makes a really strong stylistic statement in this modern farmhouse living room. The white ceiling, original shiplap walls, and neutral area rug offer a simple backdrop that plays against the black front door and bold metal accents. The darker modern furniture and black light fixture are all highlighted in a more significant way because of this contrast of colors. The furnishings and decor of this space have been edited down, which communicates that anything present—including the number 9 on the wall—is reflective of the homeowners' lives and bears significance to them.

This house is only about one thousand square feet, but it packs a lot of textures and rich details into such a tiny space. The small coffee table allows the rest of the area to be utilized for seating. I went with a modern, low-profile fireplace to help make room for a larger walkway near the sitting area. In smaller spaces like this, I often keep the furnishings and color palette simple. If I were to fill this room with a lot of stuff or add too many contrasting colors, it would feel like the walls were closing in. Instead, I chose to paint the walls white and raise the ceiling to create a more breathable living area. I also added in texture with a rug and pillows. I don't typically like to designate a theme to a home, but this house does sit on a ranch, so I complemented the clean, strong lines of the modern furniture with a few subtle, rustic details, which you'll find in the coffee table, flooring, and the antique wood staircase treads.

These homeowners have lived all over the world and they wanted their farmhouse to reflect that part of their story. In order to convey an eclectic look that combined modern and Moroccan influences, I kept the foundation of the space light and airy with white walls and window trim. I then layered in a richly toned antique area rug to anchor the room and add warmth. The round, low coffee table adds a casual vibe while the oversize sofa and placement of the two accent chairs create balance in this room, and immediately invite you in to sit and relax. The geometric light fixture helps to establish style. If you don't have an obvious focal point in your living room, consider incorporating a dramatic bookshelf to serve that purpose. I designed this one with enough shelving to display the meaningful art pieces and mementos they've collected in their travels.

When we first moved into our farmhouse, we didn't have a clear idea of how this room would function for us. It sits just off the kitchen and is somewhat secluded from the rest of the house, so it didn't feel like a natural living room. Still, it was immediately a favorite spot because of the big, beautiful windows and the original fireplace that we found hiding behind a plastered wall during demo. Unlike the rest of our living spaces, this is a separate room, so in order to contrast the white shiplap walls you see everywhere else, I painted these a rich, warm gray. It makes the space feel distinct and set apart in the best way. At first, Chip and I converted this space into an office that we could share. A few years later, it became our family den. It's where our Christmas tree has stood tall each winter, full of meaningful ornaments and lots of handmade keepsakes. Most recently, it has become a nursery for our youngest son. The life of this room is ever-changing, just like us. If you happen to have a spare room or a den, consider how your family could benefit from that extra space in this season of life and make the room serve that important purpose.

The cinder-block wall (*pages 78–79 and left*) conveys an unexpected expression of art in this living room in both pattern and texture. It fills the large two-story room with a point of interest without utilizing art or decor. The built-in shelf is inset with metal, which adds contrast and maintains the industrial feel of the house (*above*). I love the play on scale that the small art ledge above the sofa makes. The graphic use of color adds a surprising element to this space.

This traditional Tudor home has always had great bones, including the wood floors, unique trimwork, and built-ins. It all just needed to be updated. I wanted to make sure my design approach would not only preserve these architectural details but also emphasize their original character. The charcoal gray color of the inset shelves creates depth and calls attention to the ligher gray trim. The newly added beams help to define this room while also adding an extra layer of dimension. If your home lacks architectural interest, you can install exposed wood beams to the ceiling, or consider implementing unique trimwork around built-ins and cased openings.

This entire space exudes a feeling of warmth and coziness. Nothing seems to be hurried or complicated about the layered design elements in this room. In fact, the furniture itself invites you to come in and relax for a while. The lighter upholstered furnishings help soften the heavier raw materials that anchor this room, while the ceiling beams and hearth underscore the primitive style of this understated space. A few elements that are highlighted, such as the firewood stacked in the open shelves, convey the owners' preference for casual comfort.

This room combines a range of styles to achieve a look that is distinctive to the homeowners. They selected traditional tufted accent chairs that seem right at home in this primitive farmhouse aesthetic beside the handcrafted elements in this room, such as the ceiling beams and fireplace mantel. The gray-blue trim adds a nice surprise of color to the space, and the overall calming palette allows for the inherent texture and charm of this old house to shine through. If you happen to live in an old home with architectural details like this one, or have added similar finishes to your house, consider highlighting those elements by making them natural focal points in the room.

TROUBLESHOOTING

NO FOCAL POINT

A fireplace is a typical focal point, but if you don't have one in your living room, you can install a faux mantel onto your wall to serve this purpose instead. You can also use larger pieces like a hutch or bookshelf. A gallery wall of photos can also create that focal point and is a simple way to incorporate your story into the space.

LACKING VISUAL INTEREST

Adding in textiles like curtains, rugs, pillows, and throws can help warm up a bland living room and make it feel more layered. Wainscoting, antique corbels, and applied molding and trim add architectural dimension. You can also affix real or faux-wood beams to the ceiling for additional interest.

rug color and size

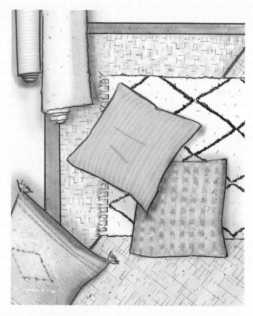

- If the majority of your living room is neutral and simple, consider a bold color or pattern in your rug. If you have a lot of pattern and color in your space already, a simple jute or natural fiber rug will make the room feel calm and cohesive. The biggest rug you can fit into a space is typically the best option, as long as you reserve a few feet around the perimeter of the room. The majority of your furniture should sit on or straddle your rug.

wall decor

- I often install antique architectural pieces, such as old gates or an interesting piece of trim that I found at a vintage market. This unconventional approach to wall decor adds dimension and makes for interesting conversation pieces.

DARK OR CAVE-LIKE

You can paint the walls and ceiling a light color to make the room feel larger. If your space lacks natural light, invest in quality lighting that will reflect well off the light-colored walls. You can also add new windows or expand existing windows to allow in more natural light. Layering in nonoverhead lighting is so important and makes a huge difference in the overall feel of a space. Floor lamps and table lamps, along with wall sconces, are effective options to create a well-lit space.

CONCEALING THE TELEVISION

If you want to place a TV in your living room, but you don't want it on display, you can install a large built-in cabinet with bi-fold doors. If your television is mounted above the fireplace, a custom mirror or large piece of artwork with a piano hinge will conceal it well. You can also hide it in a piece of furniture like an armoire if you don't want to install anything permanent.

INHERITED FURNITURE THAT'S NOT WORKING

Pieces that have been passed down can be sentimental, but may not always work with your style. If you currently have a furnishing that you can't yet replace, consider refinishing it in a stain or paint color you love. Reupholstering an old sofa or chair is an easy upgrade and allows you the opportunity to choose the fabric and color.

NO FLOW

It's smart to approach a small living room from a minimalist perspective. This will help the space feel less crowded and allow for easier movement. Consider incorporating a loveseat with side chairs instead of a large or oversize sofa. Try a round coffee table rather than a rectangular one to encourage easy flow. If you're renovating, consider creating a wall with a cased opening, which will provide sight lines between rooms and create a larger, more cohesive feel overall.

KITCHENS

Chip and I moved into our first house just after we returned home from our honeymoon. I can remember the hours I spent unpacking all of our wedding gifts and putting them away. Most of them were cooking utensils, and I spent a good deal of time choosing the perfect home for them within our bare kitchen cabinets. Before we got married, I didn't have much cooking experience at all. I picked up some things from my mom over the years, and thank goodness, because those few dishes are what got us through the first couple months of marriage. That season of life was memorable for a lot of reasons. We were newly married and living in our first home together. I had spent several months decorating each room to look just right. Back then, our kitchen was just another space to style. I really didn't feel any sort of deep connection to it. Both the room itself and all of the cooking tools that filled it felt pretty foreign to me. Part of the reason for this was because at the time, I was only cooking on a need-to basis, and on most nights just for Chip and me. I was far more interested in making this space look pretty than I was in actually using it. It wasn't until I realized the importance of what food actually meant to the two of us that I began to see the kitchen differently. Recipes that had been a part of each of our families were a comfort to us both during this new, uncharted phase of our lives. So slowly, I began to spend more time in our tiny kitchen, less by obligation and more by choice—messing with ingredients and practicing using new tools and recipes until I started to feel like I actually belonged in that space.

One of my first instincts about our kitchen involved a beautiful domed, glass cake stand we had received as a wedding gift. It's definitely no surprise to me that my first emotional connection to our kitchen involved dessert. Initially, I set the cake stand out on my counter because I thought it was pretty and worth showing off, but soon it wasn't enough that it was nice to look at. I didn't like seeing it empty. I had this desire to fill it with something good and sweet. Part of this might have been because I had an unrelenting sweet tooth—and still do—but it was also the way Chip's face would light up when he'd walk into the kitchen and see freshly baked cookies or a lemon pie waiting on the counter. Or if neighbors dropped by, they would more likely feel genuinely encouraged to stay awhile if I had something sweet to offer them. For me, that cake stand symbolized my hope that people would feel welcomed in our home. At a time when I was still learning my way around the kitchen, I understood the significance of this small act of hospitality.

When we'd have people over for a meal, I really enjoyed having them hang out with me in the kitchen while I finished cooking or prepared drinks. There wasn't enough room in there for an island, so instead I found a 3' x 3' cart with a butcher-block surface that I'd just roll in as needed. It was an awkward addition as the room really wasn't large enough for anything extra. Nonetheless, I would place it right in the middle and soon enough, people would be gathered around it eating an appetizer or resting their drinks on there. I was fascinated even then by how people innately looked for places to gather and how this quirky spot became the backdrop for the beginning of our small community of friends. Rather unexpectedly, our little kitchen became my very favorite place to be. Somewhere between the new neighbor leaning against the kitchen counter as we talked and laughed and ate pie, and those nights huddled with friends around that tiny butcher-block cart, our kitchen became the heartbeat of our home.

Once we started flipping houses, we were moving so often that I never stayed in one kitchen for too long. But from then on, my cake stand remained full of something sweet, and over the next few years, no matter the house we were living in, I continued to pull out that same 3' x 3' cart for dinner parties. These two inanimate objects came to symbolize ideals of anticipating hospitality and creating spaces for gathering that have continued to guide my overall design philosophy through the years.

When I was working on making design plans for the kitchens in the first few houses that we flipped, I was determined to make them look beautiful despite the very limited budgets I was working within. I approached these renovations thinking about the space only from a cosmetic standpoint and I dreamed about what I could add to make them really stand out. My primary focus was making these kitchens aesthetically pleasing, and if I got lucky, functional as well. In those early days, functionality just never seemed to me a worthwhile enough priority. As I became more proficient in my own kitchen, it started to alter my design approach. Now with any kitchen design, there are two things I always consider before I begin: the functionality of the space and how to make it inspiring for the people who use it every day.

In our farmhouse, the kitchen is open to the living room as well as the dining room. This floor plan works well for us because these three rooms all exist within a relatively small footprint. This open flow, while not for everyone, is important to us because it really supports how our family actually functions day to day. We have a big family and everyone likes to gather around our island not only at mealtimes but also throughout the day just to hang out. I'm usually cooking dinner when the kids settle in at the island or dining table to do their homework, so it works well for us to have this space where we can talk to one another. We utilize our kitchen in a bunch of different ways, so it has naturally become the setting for many of the everyday moments we share as a family. We spend so much of our lives in this one spot that it needed to be comfortable and welcoming and thoughtfully laid out.

There's an old adage about how the kitchen is the heart of the home, and as trite as that may sound, there's obviously a reason it became a cliché in the first place. Food is our family's love language, for Chip and me for sure, but for the kids even more so. I can already imagine that twenty years from now, our kitchen will be the first place they settle in when they come home for a visit, and that hours will pass by as we're all gathered around that island, just as we do today. That's my wish for this space.

If you feel drawn to this same idea of having those you love gathered in your kitchen, make that your priority in this space. Determine whether you can build in an island, and if you can't, consider a movable cart like the one I used to roll in. It served us well for a lot of years, and even though I now have a good-size island like the one I wished for back then, the moments that we spent around that cart were just as rich as the ones we have now. Opening up my kitchen to family and friends is the best way I know how to show them that they are an important part of my life and that they are loved. Whether I'm alone and unhurried, playing with new recipes in a quiet kitchen or it's noisy and full of the people I love, this room is a gift to me, and well, nothing else comes close to embodying just what I want from my home.

(*Page 90*) My priority in our kitchen is that it be incredibly functional for our family. The marble countertop on the island is practical for baking, and the concrete counters are durable, while also adding contrast to this primarily white space. The island is an antique piece that once sat in an old church and it's now the primary focal point in our kitchen. The oversize subway tile backsplash keeps the space feeling bright and airy. (*Page 93*) The clean-lined metal open shelving is a modern element that balances the distressed textures of the room. The black metal draws your eyes up and offers a nice contrast to the white walls. (*Above*) Cookbooks and everyday ingredients are kept close by for easy reference on this baker's rack. A few family heirlooms are on display, including my grand-pa's Syrian doughnut recipe. I love having this meaningful item in a place where I can see it every day.

CRITICAL
THINKING

IN DESIGN

KITCHENS:
WHAT TO CONSIDER

The kitchen is typically where you'll see the highest financial return on your investment. It's often the most fundamental room in the house, so it's understandable why most home-owners choose to invest their money and time here. Whether you're considering simple updates or a complete remodel of your kitchen, you should approach this space in terms of making it not only highly functional, but also a beautiful, welcoming place to gather.

WHAT'S ON DISPLAY

- Notice how the spaces in this chapter display everyday items on countertops and shelves in a beautiful and practical way.

NEUTRAL PALETTE

- The kitchens featured in this chapter all boast a relatively neutral color palette, where textiles and accessories contribute subtle hints of color.

MIXED MATERIALS

- Notice the blend of materials in these kitchens, from metal open shelving to glass cabinets.

THE ELEMENTS

- CABINET UPGRADES
- ATTRACTIVE BARSTOOLS
- CHOPPING BLOCK
- OPEN SHELVING
- ISLAND OR PENINSULA
- POTTED PLANTS
- TASK LIGHTING

- POT FILLER
- UPDATED HARDWARE
- COLORFUL COOKBOOKS
- PATTERNED BACKSPLASH
- SPICE JARS
- POT RACK
- DECORATIVE KITCHEN MAT

This kitchen, full of contrast and distinctive flooring, blends practicality and design well. The island is stocked full of key ingredients and supplies for easy accessibility. The homeowner has utilized trays to keep items that stay out on the countertops both organized and attractive. If you don't have a built-in island, but you do have a few spare feet in your kitchen, consider adding a small table or cart to function as a working island and increase countertop space.

In order to blend the rustic and modern styles that these homeowners loved in this kitchen, I incorporated both wood tones as well as clean-lined elements. Instead of a typical tile backsplash, I chose a streamlined and modern marble stone slab with veining that makes an elevated statement. I'm a fan of open shelving but also have an appreciation for closed cabinets. This kitchen shows how to blend the best of both worlds. Pieces that serve a functional purpose like this simple wall-hanging pot rack can also make a strong design statement.

This homeowner converted two pre-existing spaces in what was formerly a duplex into one amazing kitchen. Rich colors and warm wood hues are blended within a more traditional white-and-black palette, creating both a classic and eclectic look. Despite the fusing of two homes into one, this space wasn't taken down to its studs. Instead, the cabinetry and tile were updated to match each other. New upper cabinets were built with traditional glass doors, framing both sinks for a classic symmetrical look. The lower cabinets and island are painted a deep black, adding a nice contrast to the white upper cabinets and the island's marble countertop.

This was at one time an empty corner that sat at the far end of the kitchen. If left alone, this would have been a few feet of unused space. But the homeowner wanted to utilize every inch of her kitchen, so she converted this bare corner into a coffee bar that now gets plenty of use every morning. The wooden bar and marble backsplash tie in seamlessly with the rest of the kitchen.

I wanted this kitchen at Hillcrest Estate to feel classic and warm. I intentionally mixed brass tones with cooler gray cabinets to give it a modern edge within a more traditional setting. This is a good-size kitchen, but because it's most often used by vacationing families and needed to be functional for larger groups, I attached a peninsula to the brick wall framing out the stove to add additional seating and a serving area.

This kitchen design was inspired by the homeowners' modern taste and love of brass elements. The black cabinets, waterfall island, and hardware offer a dramatic look. Because large windows provide a lot of natural light, the black cabinets don't make the space feel too dark. I offset the moody color with light marble on both of the countertops and the backsplash. The nearby bartop offers additional seating and a great view of the beautiful wooded backyard.

This kitchen is in a tiny ranch house, so I incorporated mostly white materials, including the upper and lower cabinets and tile backsplash, to make the space feel bigger and blend seamlessly with the rest of the rooms in this open floor plan. To give the kitchen character, I added in natural textures with the irregular clay tiles used for the backsplash and the concrete counters. These handcrafted elements complement the modern style of the hardware, light fixture, and bold metal vent hood.

These homeowners chose to utilize one entire wall of their kitchen for large windows, which has made way for a ton of natural light to fill this room. Since this is a smaller space, the open shelving is functional and also makes the area appear more spacious. The unrefined elements of the kitchen—from the wood countertop to the industrial beams and exposed ductwork— reflect the urban lifestyle of the homeowners. The visible bike storage is yet another layer of personalization, showing that they've created a home that is tailored to their interests.

In this kitchen, high function meets sleek design. The vaulted wood-planked ceiling and similarly toned floor juxtapose the industrial cabinetry and utilitarian design, adding warmth to what could feel like a sterile space. The warm wood seats and metal legs of the bar stools also reflect this blend of styles. Stainless steel cabinetry and appliances offer a durable and utilitarian element to the kitchen, while also bringing in an industrial look.

The kitchen island, vaulted oak ceiling beams, and matching pocket doors create a cohesive look while the patterned tile backsplash provides a lot of visual interest within a relatively small setting. If there is a pricey material that you love but you can't afford to use it generously, choose a small, high-impact spot like this to feature it without spending a lot. The built-in double-sided hutch (*above*) adds another layer of personality, constructed with the same oak wood and cremone bolts used throughout the space. It also serves this room functionally as additional storage and serving space.

I wanted this kitchen to feel bold and classic—two characteristics that define the rest of this home. Raw wood is a simple way to add a casual, distinctive look to an otherwise traditional or modern space, and mixing these warm wood tones with the black cabinets and white-tiled backsplash laid in varying patterns creates a unique, eclectic style.

The stone walls with German Smear backsplash, a technique that involves applying wet mortar to stone or brick, give this kitchen an old-world feel, ideal for its rustic ranch setting. Concrete countertops and sleek wood cabinets add a modern edge, while the copper accents are a warm, classic addition. Oftentimes, dead space on the backside of an island can be an ideal area to display cookbooks. Look for other spots in your kitchen where additional storage can be carved out.

I am not afraid,
I was made for this.

- Joan of Arc

The overall design of this urban loft is industrial, allowing for the few significant style choices to really stand out. The use of black and white materials makes a bold statement, but when paired with light wood floors and brass hardware, the feeling of the room is transformed from high contrast and potentially sterile to warm and inviting. In order to ensure that the kitchen blends seamlessly with the rest of the space, I added industrial elements, including the metal vent hood, light fixtures, and a stainless-steel mobile island.

This kitchen strikes an ideal balance of texture and style. Painting just one wall in this otherwise neutral space makes a significant aesthetic statement, as does the simple beauty of antique cooking utensils hung beneath the vent hood.

From the collection of art hung on the wall to the unique cabinet design beneath the sink, these homeowners were intent on incorporating only the details they loved in their kitchen. This space is a great example of less is more—there is nothing displayed that isn't serving a purpose or bringing joy to the people who use this space every day.

TROUBLESHOOTING

NOT ENOUGH STORAGE

Free up valuable cabinet or drawer space by utilizing creative storage solutions such as utensil holders, wall hooks for kitchen textiles and tools, and pot racks.

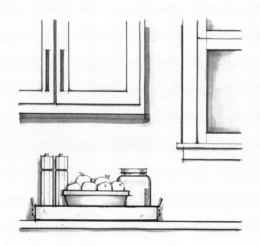

LACKING COUNTER SPACE

If your kitchen feels cluttered or you prefer a minimal look, clear your counters of everything but the essentials. You can use trays or cutting boards to keep items that stay out on the countertops organized. If you have the space, add a small table that can function as a working island. This will increase valuable countertop space. You can purchase stainless steel work and storage tables from restaurant supply stores, or find an antique one.

INSUFFICIENT TASK LIGHTING

Sufficient light is essential in the kitchen. If your space is dark, hire an electrician to install a hanging pendant, chandelier, recessed cans, or under-cabinet task lighting.

EXPOSED APPLIANCES

Install your microwave into an island, or stash it away in the pantry or a cabinet along with any other small appliances that aren't used every day. You may need an electrician to install an extra outlet in these spaces. Cabinets can also be customized to hide refrigerators or dishwashers.

OUTDATED KITCHEN

Changing the paint color or hardware on your cabinets are small updates that can make a huge difference in your kitchen. If you're wanting a new style altogether, consider hiring a cabinet-maker to replace the doors and drawer fronts. Glass doors are also a beautiful choice in a kitchen. You can frame an area like the sink or the cooktop/range with these for a traditional look. You can also paint your lower cabinets, or island if you have one, a contrasting color and keep the uppers white for added visual interest. Updating the flooring or backsplash tile can also change the entire look and feel of a kitchen.

upgrading hardware

- For a simple replacement, like switching out handles, you can measure the length of the existing handle and shop around for new ones that match that size. If you want to change up the size and look of your handles completely, apply wood filler to the existing holes, and sand it down evenly once dry. Then, drill holes to your new measurements and lightly sand the whole door. To finish, add a fresh coat of paint for an updated look.

replacing cabinetry

- If you want to replace your cabinetry altogether, you have the flexibility to reimagine the layout and look of your entire kitchen.

open shelving

- If you love the look and ease of open shelving, tear out your existing upper cabinets to make space for this relatively easy upgrade. Choose from a range of styles, including wood, metal, or glass as well as the type of look you'd like, such as floating or bracketed shelves. With any style, be prepared to texture and paint the wall. Also make sure there is sufficient stud support to hold up the shelving.

DINING ROOMS

There's something about settling in around the dining room table that feels important. While the kitchen island works well for snacks or lunch, dinner happens at our table. It feels like the most significant part of the day to us. On most nights, it's where we gather once everyone is home for the evening and we have nowhere else to be. In the midst of our busy lives and scattered schedules, a leisurely meal around the table is just what we all need to feel grounded. As the kids are getting older, our conversations are getting richer. Nowadays, it seems that we all tend to eat a little slower and no one is in a hurry to leave the table.

I really appreciate what this room represents. It's a set-apart space that has been intentionally designated for lingering over good food and conversation with family and friends. I want anyone who gathers in our dining room to feel welcomed and comfortable. We have this saying displayed on a wall at our restaurant: "Where everyone has a seat at the table." I mean this just as much for our restaurant guests as I do for anyone who sits around our table at home. When I think about this space in terms of balancing comfort with this more meaningful purpose, I get really excited about how certain design choices can help turn these ideals of hospitality into reality.

Our dining room happens to share a space with the kitchen as well as the living room, so it's not really a formally defined space. Still, I wanted to be intentional about its placement in a way that could give it the significance it deserves. Long before we actually bought our farmhouse, we'd sometimes take a drive out to see the property. The owner was always kind enough to let the kids run wild while Chip and I sat beneath one of the oak trees that towered over the backyard. My favorite part about those visits was the enormous trees that sheltered us as we hoped and planned for our future. Once the house was ours, I decided to position our large dining table in a place where we could look out at those billowing oak trees that I've loved for so long. To me, even though this space lacks definition and doesn't allow for a ton of extra design elements, that's okay. It is made unique by having a front-row seat to the best view in the house. Now, whenever I look out the window from the dining room table, I still remember those early days and all the dreams they held.

It's pretty standard for older homes to have both a formal dining area as well as a smaller breakfast nook near the kitchen. That was certainly the trend in residential construction for many years, when more and bigger was better. These days, many of our clients prefer to have just one dining space in

an effort to maximize the functionality of their house. I love to hear this from clients as I, too, am all about utilizing every square inch of our home to its fullest potential.

If your house has more than one dining space, think about transforming one of these areas into something you would use more often. If you have a formal dining room that you rarely sit in, consider giving it a new purpose and build out your breakfast nook to serve as your primary dining area instead. This can work both ways. Perhaps it's the formal space that remains while the nook becomes an extra sitting area or a useful coffee bar. When considering these types of changes, whatever makes the most sense for your family is really all that should matter.

I think you'll find the greatest value in a dining room that's as functional for everyday meals as it is for formal occasions worthy of the holidays. Many people struggle to move past the idea that dining rooms should look fancy and only be used for the finer moments, but I can't help but fight for a room that serves both of these purposes well. Typically, the rooms that are reserved for use only a few times a year just don't have the same level of warmth and life as a space that's truly lived in.

This room, no matter how often or scarcely you use it, should look and feel like your family year-round, just as much as any other space might. This is where you enjoy good food and conversation. It should never feel plain or muted or uninspiring. In fact, since this space is typically closed off or sep-

arated from the main gathering areas of the house, it affords a fun opportunity to be a bit more creative. Perhaps it's with wallpaper that you love but feel is too bold to put anywhere else. Maybe it's a whimsical light fixture or cool artwork. Anything that speaks to you that might seem too dramatic, or just different from the primary tone of the house, could be perfect here. The dining room is a great spot to just go for it.

If your dining area is more like mine and shares a space with other living quarters, I recommend choosing textures and colors that complement the rest of the area so that there's a consistent flow within the space as a whole. Rather than reaching for bold colors or textiles that could make the space feel disjointed, look for chairs that are both beautiful and comfortable and a dining table that works well with your typical crowd.

Kitchens and dining rooms go hand in hand for me, and are two of my favorite places to be. But unlike the busyness that tends to fill a room meant for food preparation, the dining room feels quite the opposite. There, just by taking a seat, I feel prompted to slow down and simply enjoy the people I'm surrounded by. It's never the actual meal that makes our time together matter, it's what happens when everyone chooses to linger at the table long after the dessert plates have been cleared. When our kids do eventually excuse themselves or our guests head home, we want them to leave full—not just from the food, but from the experience they had around our table.

(Page 138 and above) Our dining room shares a space with our kitchen and living room, so I kept the look consistent by mixing styles that are used throughout our open floor plan. The distressed farmhouse table is the focal point here, and it sits well beside the shiplap walls and nearby antique kitchen island. The clean-lined leather chairs provide a modern contrast to the antique chandelier that ties it all together and helps establish this spot as the dining area. *(Page 140)* I love to incorporate found pieces that have some history into my house. The distressed green color of this vintage jewelry cabinet is one of my favorites. Clearly I'm drawn to this tone, because it also shows up in the "Pharmacie" sign that hangs in the kitchen and the antique piano in the living room.

CRITICAL
THINKING
IN DESIGN

DINING ROOMS:
WHAT TO CONSIDER

What you'll find in this chapter are dining rooms that feel significant and intentional, whether they're used twice a year or every day. The actual furnishings that fill these spaces tend to be few, but the components featured in this chapter cross all styles and genres of design.

KEEP IT CONSISTENT OR MAKE IT DISTINCT

- Dining spaces that happen to be located right off the kitchen or as part of an open floor plan, like mine, will typically feature design elements that are consistent with the larger context of the area they share. In these spaces, a focal point such as a table or dramatic light fixture can help establish the space as the dining room.

- If your dining room is separated from the rest of the house, look closely at how the homes featured in this chapter set the room apart. Typically, separate dining rooms will feature a few significant design elements that make the space feel distinct, like a large hutch or mirror, a bolder wall color, or a textured or patterned rug.

- Consider how textiles, including window treatments, cushions, placemats, and rugs can help to soften the space.

THE ELEMENTS

- SPACIOUS AND STURDY TABLE
- COMFORTABLE SEATING
- STATEMENT LIGHT FIXTURE
- DRAMATIC WALLPAPER
- VERSATILE CENTERPIECE
- INTERESTING ARTWORK
- CANDLES AND CANDLESTICKS
- HUTCH OR BUFFET

I added black built-ins to make a strong statement in this formal dining room, and the paneling behind the shelves resonates with the antique charm of this historical estate. To reach a balance of bold and casual, and to lighten up the aesthetic of the space, I incorporated antique pine dining chairs and white serveware on the shelves. The dramatic beaded chandelier offers an element of grandiosity hung above the oversize double-pedestal dining table. The garland of greenery on the fireplace mantel stands out against the all-black architecture, creating both contrast and an organic element that softens the overall look.

Floor-to-ceiling windows offer a great view of the backyard from this open-concept kitchen and dining area. The simple black dining table and surprisingly comfortable white chairs look right at home within this modern space. The unique, understated light fixture helps to define the dining space and blends in enough that it doesn't detract from the main attraction: the view.

A lot of styles are brought together in this dining room. The industrial seating and dual light fixtures are balanced by a vintage area rug and ornate mirror. Since this area is right off the living room, the rug helps to make this spot feel anchored and significant in its own right. It also adds a lot of color and warmth to this otherwise neutral space.

I balanced the white walls and light terrazzo floors of this dining room with subtle design features to create an interesting contrast of materials and color. The black-and-white vintage maps of the homeowners' city add a strong graphic element and personalization to this space. Something as simple as replacing an old chandelier with a modern alternative completely changed the feel of this entire room, suddenly reframing all of the other pieces in the space in an entirely new light. The bar seating (*above*) is adjacent to the dining room and overlooks the wooded backyard, and for large gatherings, this spot functions as additional seating.

This dining space sits right off the kitchen, and because the square footage of this house is tiny, I installed booth seating to maximize space. The diner-style benches, built from antique threshing-wood flooring, bring in the ranch style that is inherent to the setting of this house. Metal black windows contribute to the overall industrial aesthetic used throughout the home and filter in plenty of natural light throughout the day.

This is the type of dining room you can hang out in for hours without ever caring how much time has passed. This room balances light and dark so well. The charcoal-black wall color and dark wood flooring exude a sense of coziness, and because there is a substantial amount of natural light coming in through the bay window, the moodiness isn't overpowering. This bold paint choice is perfectly juxtaposed with the light art on the wall and the dining chairs that surround the table, a few of which are family heirlooms.

The wood and leather in this dining room contrast well with the lighter walls (*pages 158–159*), creating a rustic yet elegant look. I incorporated selections of pewter, plants, and hand-thrown ceramic dishes on the open shelves to lighten up the substantial wooden furniture. What you display on open shelving in your kitchen or dining room is oftentimes practical and utilitarian. Mixing in a few unexpected or storied pieces to otherwise neutral arrangements adds an interesting layer to the shelves.

This space reflects both the midcentury architecture and southwest elements used throughout the house. The dining table and seating both have a modern bent while the Saltillo flooring brings in a southwest vibe. These two styles are bridged together by the rustic framed photos on the gallery wall, and easily work well together in this space because they share a warm, natural color palette.

The blend of old and new gives this dining room a unique, timeless look that I just love. The antique table paired with structured metal chairs makes the biggest impact. As an alternative to replacing uncomfortable chairs, just add removable seat cushions in a neutral shade for an easy upgrade to both comfort and style. The gray wainscoting and trim partnered with brass accents give a fresh interpretation to the historical detailing of the room.

TROUBLESHOOTING

LACKING AMBIANCE

lighting

- When choosing a chandelier, think about the scale of the room as well as the ceiling height. Typically, a chandelier can safely hang 26" to 36" above the table. If you have a longer table, consider hanging two larger pendant lights above it. Recessed cans will bring in additional light if your space needs it, or you can install dimmer switches, which allow you to set the level of light in the room to your liking.

wall color

- Bold or rich wall colors can intensify the mood of this space, while lighter, neutral tones bring a brighter vibe. Consider incorporating wallpaper in your dining room for an even bigger statement.

textiles

- Add curtains or a rug to soften and add warmth to the room.

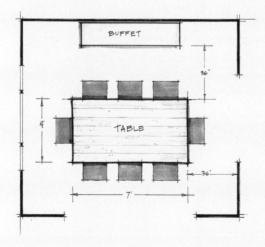

TABLE SIZE AND SCALE

Select a table size and shape that maximizes seating and ensures ease of movement around your table. Determine what shape of table will work best in the room—oval, circle, square, or rectangular. If possible, leave at least 36" between the edge of your table and other furniture or the wall. This allows enough room for someone to pass through behind the chairs while everyone is seated.

NO SEPARATE DINING ROOM

If you don't have a dining room, get creative and find a spot that you can carve out for this purpose. You can define the space with lighting and furniture, such as an oversize or interesting chandelier or a substantial table. Banquette seating or built-in benches can also bring some functionality to the space.

UNCOMFORTABLE SEATING

If you want people to linger around your table and stay awhile, choose comfortable seating that will make your dining room more inviting. There are so many options out there that are both beautiful and comfortable. Don't be afraid to mix and match styles for a gathered or eclectic look.

ADD DIMENSION

- Add architectural interest with trimwork around doors, windows, ceilings, and floors. You can take this further with wainscoting or applied wall paneling.

- Walls aren't the only place you can add dimension. Ceilings can be treated with shiplap, decorative medallions, embossed ceiling tiles, and exposed or coffered beams.

- Windows can also be highlighted with plantation shutters or window treatments.

- Built-in cabinetry can be added to enhance the space through form and function. This is an ideal place to display or store glassware, silverware, and serving pieces.

- In lieu of architectural additions that require construction, wallpaper can add a similar effect through texture, pattern, and color. Grasscloth paper is a great option if you are specifically looking to add texture over pattern. Peel-and-stick wallpaper options are also available if you don't want to make a permanent change.

BEDROOMS

Mornings at the farm are quiet and tranquil. We have no city lights or street sounds to nudge us from our sweet slumber. On most days, we wake up just before the sun does, only because that's when our rooster starts to crow. Chip and I try to leave our cell phones charging in the den when we go to bed at night so that we can start each day on our own terms. Sometimes we forget or fail to do this, but we really try to be deliberate about boundaries when it comes to what we let infringe on our time. For Chip and me, it's important that we keep our bedroom as a sort of sanctuary, an escape from the busyness of life. We want to put our best foot forward from the start of the day and peacefully sink into bed at night, so we try to remove any distractions that don't help that cause. I like to envision that a line is drawn at the base of our bedroom door frame, separating our space from the things that feel like diversions—our work, our chores, our devices. Leaving those things on the other side of that line is how we clock out. While a lot of those things are good and important, they are not *more* important than taking the time to unwind and truly rest.

Early in our marriage, Chip and I were on a pretty tight budget, so we spent most evenings at home. We didn't have the cash to eat out a lot so we stayed in and cooked instead. We'd typically spend the rest of the night working on a project together or doing something as simple as playing cards. We found ourselves hanging out in the living room more than anywhere else, but that space always felt full of distractions and reminders of things that needed to get done, whether it be a stack of mail or items out of place. We both wanted a space that felt separate from all of that, and somewhat unconsciously we fell into a rhythm of seeking out our bedroom for refuge and for time spent together. Almost immediately, there was this silent agreement between us that work wouldn't follow us into that space. It became a well-worn pattern of how we lived, which in turn caused me to really think through how the design of this space could help facilitate these intentions.

At the time, the setup of our room wasn't ideal in light of all the time we started to spend there. Really, this space had been an afterthought when we first moved in. I had spent all of my creative energy on the more visible rooms of the house so that our home looked finished and presentable to others. This meant that our bedroom received the leftover furniture that I hadn't liked enough to use in the main living area. When guests came over, I would just shut our bedroom door so I didn't have to explain why it wasn't finished.

Gradually, though, Chip's and my tendencies were teaching me more about design than I ever could have learned any other way. Our bedroom was important to our relationship and our ability to connect. So, slowly it evolved from being an afterthought to a priority, and I began to create a space that felt like a retreat from the outside world.

I wanted our bedroom to feel separate enough from the rest of the house that we would be prompted at the door to quiet our minds and really relax. For the first time, I was able to see how impersonal a lot of our mismatched furniture was. The secondhand furnishings communicated that this room was less important than the other, more visible parts of our house. The full laundry hamper that sat beside our nightstand was a reminder of a never-ending chore waiting to be done. These things felt contrary to what had become the clear intent of this space. It was then that I decided we'd keep only the furniture that we loved, and I became pretty critical about what we kept out in the open. I placed items like that laundry basket in the closet and moved the catchall to the entryway. And for a long time we lived with a half-furnished room, but half-furnished with pieces that meant something to us. That bedroom, so imperfect and in process, felt just like us. And for that season of life, it was just right.

One weekend, Chip and I scored a couple of beautiful old leather chairs from an estate sale for a great price. I placed these comfortable chairs in a corner by the window in our bedroom, and they were the perfect addition. As simple as they were, those chairs were really significant in helping Chip and me to unwind and connect. In every house we've lived in since, I've always placed a pair of chairs in our bedroom. Sometimes they were crammed into the corner of a really small room where there really wasn't space for these two large pieces, but we didn't care. By that point they'd come to mean too much to us to live without them.

Over the years, our tendency to hang out in our bedroom has never faded, which has made me feel all the more compelled to make this space all about Chip and me. I began to place things in our room that were meaningful only to us. Old letters and small mementos became the invaluable pieces that I hung as art and arranged on shelves. These served as reminders of where we've been and what we hold dear, helping to keep us grounded and really making this space feel sacred. Details I wouldn't display in other rooms of the house were perfect in our bedroom because they helped to tell our story as a couple. This is the one place that's for us and no one else.

That's what I enjoy most about working on bedrooms. It is the room that has the best opportunity to use design to communicate an individual's preferences with details from his or her life. When I design a client's bedroom, I pay particular attention to the things they find interesting. The colors, patterns, and styles that they gravitate toward or their hobbies and places they've traveled lead me to choose materials and pieces that I know will bring them comfort and peace.

In any room, but particularly in the bedroom, it is important that the space feel restful and not chaotic. Clearing away clutter and nonessentials really can promote peace. This room should be the one place that you can count on to provide you with the rest you need to feel renewed. When your bedroom shelters you from the worries of the world while making room for the things that energize you to get back up and tackle another day, that is how you know that you are home.

(*Pages 168–171*) I wanted our bedroom to feel like a true retreat, so I incorporated a soft, peaceful color palette with cozy textures, traditional shapes, and sophisticated finishes. The cream wall color is warm in tone and the plush blue accents add a sense of calm. A chandelier hung above our bed brings some definition to this wide open space. (*Page 173*) This antique card catalog–style dresser adds a sense of story to the traditional and modern elements of the room, and the large botanical artwork hung above ties in with the vintage academic vibe. (*Above*) This quiet corner adds to the retreat-like feel of the room. Outfitted with a writer's desk and minimal decor, this spot is ideal for quiet time and reflection.

CRITICAL
THINKING
IN DESIGN

BEDROOMS: WHAT TO CONSIDER

Our bedroom should be a place that provides us with rest and refuge. One that actually feels like a breath of fresh air typically requires deliberate efforts to edit out any meaningless items and nonessential pieces that take up precious space. The rooms in this chapter have all been designed and styled minimally, making the pieces that are on display feel significant and a reflection of the stories and personalities of the people who live in them.

COMPLEMENTARY ARRANGEMENT

- Consider how the size, shape, and arrangement of furniture contribute to the flow of the bedrooms shared in this chapter. Typically, I style clients' bedrooms by sticking to the basics with a bed, dresser, rug, and two nightstands when space allows. This needn't mean that the bedroom should look or feel bland or generic. The select few pieces of furniture you do choose should reflect your personal sense of style and complement the shape and size of the room, while leaving plenty of space to relax.

DETAILS MATTER

- Pay attention to what your eyes are drawn to in each room. For me, it's typically a bold or unique bed, layered with interesting textiles. This is why I recommend investing in a quality frame and bedding if you can. Linens that feel as comfortable as they look beautiful are a worthwhile investment. The bedroom is a great place to highlight mementos, artwork, and personal photos that celebrate a life well lived.

THE ELEMENTS

- BENCH OR CHAISE LOUNGE
- PERSONAL ARTWORK
- ADJUSTABLE BEDSIDE LIGHTING
- ARMOIRE OR WRITING DESK
- COMFORTABLE BEDDING

- QUALITY BED FRAME
- SIDE TABLES
- CATCHALL OR VALET TRAY
- SOFT AREA RUG
- WINDOW TREATMENT

You can refine your bedroom by establishing a simplified color palette for the space. For example, this room is defined by neutral tones with accent hues of green and blue, found in the art prints, potted plants, and books. The muted bedding and jute rug also help to smooth out the dark lines of the furniture for a beautiful blend within a traditional style.

The live-edge headboard is the design highlight of this guest bedroom. Since it is such a unique and organic piece of furniture, the other pieces I incorporated are sleek and understated, like the modern light fixture and the small metal shelf in lieu of a nightstand. I added a small side porch off this room with a wall of sliding doors so that guests could enjoy the view or an early-morning cup of coffee.

In this master bedroom, traditional farmhouse features like the board-and-batten accent wall are balanced with industrial elements, including the black metal bed frame and copper light fixtures. To achieve a simplified and clean feeling in this room, I kept the decor to a minimum, and chose neutral art prints that would subtly blend with the rest of the room. Instead of traditional nightstands, I opted for narrow side tables to better suit this relatively tight space.

Instead of using a traditional headboard in this industrial downtown loft bedroom, I incorporated a wood-paneled half wall. This unconventional headboard not only complements the style of the home, it also doubles as a shelf for books, layered art, and plants. In a relatively neutral room, a bold-colored rug will not only ground the space but also provide plenty of color.

The textured rug, throw blankets, and paneled ceiling add layers of visual interest to this crisp and clean-styled bedroom. I balanced the quirky angles of the ceiling with the symmetrical placement of the twin beds and sconces. Since it is a small space, I kept the color palette simple by using mostly neutrals with a subtle addition of yellow. A little bit of black goes a long way toward helping a space like this one convey a modern sensibility in a country aesthetic.

Simple, natural design was the inspiration for this loft bedroom. The warm wood tones, neutral textiles, and vaulted ceiling offer an organic and raw aesthetic that is complemented by a practical and understated floating wood shelf in lieu of a larger piece of furniture.

When I designed this room, it was intended to be a quiet retreat for a writer. The clean, natural palette offers minimal distractions, and is ideal for cultivating creativity. There are few spaces that wouldn't benefit from adding a couple of potted plants. They instantly bring warmth, life, and movement to a room. To me, plants are the easiest and happiest quick fix for any spot.

(*Opposite*) If a bold or unique paint color seems intimidating for the bedroom, wallpaper can be an excellent option for adding some personality. This unique wallpaper choice makes a statement about the couple's fun and original style. Matching furniture, along with calming, neutral textiles with subtle textures, ensures a sense of balance. (*Above*) A gallery of abstract art anchors the wall opposite the bold, papered accent wall.

PHOTOGRAPHY
THE DEFINITIVE VISUAL HISTORY

WONDERS OF THE WORLD edited by Francesca Bottia

To highlight the historical architecture of this Hillcrest Estate bedroom, I refinished the original built-in bookshelf and desk. I created a moody aesthetic and highlighted the masculinity of the space by painting the walls a dark blue. I typically try to strike a nice balance between masculine and feminine elements in every room. Here, the botanical prints and the movement of the linen bed skirt help balance the masculinity of the rest of this bedroom.

This cinder-block wall continues to play an important stylistic role throughout this house, including in the bedroom. True to industrial style, these homeowners have creatively re-purposed this urban material to serve as a nightstand, allowing for fewer furnishings in this space. If you're building something new, consider working an inset structure like this one into your design plans. It can be both a significant and functional design statement. The unique wall pairs well with the bold color of the window drapes—a reminder that it only takes one unexpected choice to make a room come alive.

I love when a bedroom features pieces that are important to the people who use them every day. The chest at the foot of this bed is a family heirloom, and the unique wood nightstand was cut from the homeowner's property, just for this purpose. The substantial pieces in this bedroom, including the metal bed frame, jute rug, and wood accents, vary in style, yet they work well together in this space because they are all in a similarly unrefined, raw state.

The original architectural details of this bedroom are the first things that catch my eye. The antiques that fill the space, including the nightstand, writing desk, and turned-wood bed frame, create a cozy atmosphere and a sense of historical importance. The neutral palette and minimal decor allow the wide-planked floors and exposed wooden beams to be the standout features of this primitive bedroom.

TROUBLESHOOTING

INSUFFICIENT STORAGE

If your space allows, select bedside tables with drawers for maximum storage space. In the absence of a large closet, bring in an armoire, dresser, or chest of drawers that can help the cause. I have four large plastic bins where I like to store extra linens and blankets under my bed year-round.

SMALL SPACE

If you don't have a ton of extra square footage in your bedroom, you can opt for floating nightstands in place of standing furniture. A built-in headboard or low-profile bed frame can take up less visible space, while losing the footboard will save you a few extra inches of floor room.

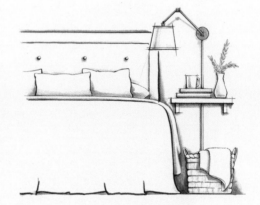

OUTDATED CARPET

If your bedroom carpet is outdated, consider replacing it with a newer style you like. You can also place a large area rug on top of the carpet in a color and pattern that gives your bedroom character. A rug is usually one of the first details I add to a client's bedroom, and it's amazing how this one piece can easily bring a room to life and help establish the overall design of the space. An alternative option is laminate or wood flooring, which will give your room a lighter look.

LACKING PERSONALITY

Your bed and bedding can be your biggest investment in this space. Once you have those in place, everything else you layer in should be complementary and draw your attention back to this main focal point. Adding a decorative wall sconce or lamp to each side of the bed will add dimension, interest, and light. You can also bring in some colorful detail by painting or wallpapering an accent wall. Putting art you love in your bedroom is a great way to make the space feel personal.

BARE WINDOWS

Window treatments can provide privacy, texture, and detail to a space. I typically choose them in neutral colors so that they can serve as a subtle backdrop to the room. You can select from many options, including blackout curtains, a pleated or panel style, roman shades, and plantation shutters. To make your windows appear larger, hang curtains a few inches above the trim.

NO PLACE TO RETREAT

Add a chaise lounge, chair, or window seat with a cushion for relaxing. A bench at the end of the bed also offers a nice spot to land.

07

BATHROOMS

Typically, I don't shy away from a challenge. I find myself really motivated to do the very things that I am told will be too hard or simply can't be done. I haven't always taken on risk so willingly, though. In fact, before I met Chip I avoided uncertainty in all of its forms—especially anything I didn't know for sure that I could do well. But I married a man who thrives on taking on experiences that most people run away from.

I think Chip's unique perspective took root in my own thinking when we started flipping houses. Our remodeling budget was always slim. The properties were small and inexpensive and we needed to ensure that we could get the best possible return on our investment. That meant I had to get creative about making affordable improvements and updates on these houses that would not only make them more beautiful but also add to the value of the property. Chip's enthusiasm for untapped potential lit a fire in me, which fueled my confidence to trust my instincts and just go for it. Before long, we were scheming together about how we could complete each new project faster and better than the one before.

When we started taking on renovations for clients, my love for a challenge only strengthened. But I began to realize that

not everyone is wired like Chip and me and motivated in the same ways that we are. Many of the clients who were hiring us to renovate their homes were allocating the bulk of their budget to their main living spaces, which left little money for secondary spaces. They seemed immobilized by what to do with any additional rooms or square footage they weren't yet able to fit into their renovation budget. This was and is most often the case for bathrooms.

We watched so many of our clients struggle with how to work around the bland and outdated look of this space. Very often they refused to invest *anything* into their bathrooms until they could properly gut and remodel the entire thing.

By this point, Chip and I had become very familiar with the "too many rooms, not enough dollars" equation. But here's the thing: the bathroom isn't a place that you can hide from or simply shut the door and ignore. Any room in which we begin and end our day deserves some serious attention.

When our clients would tell us their plans to postpone the bathroom until they could fully fund a complete remodel, I couldn't help but think that their problem wasn't all about design. It may have been more about perspective. To me, these

bathrooms presented a fun and important challenge. I convinced many of them to let me attempt to give their bathrooms a simple, painless update—*for less than a hundred bucks.* They'd usually agree, though with a healthy dose of skepticism, confident that there was no way their outdated bathroom could be transformed into something they'd love at such a low cost.

Details and display are the unsung heroes of compact spaces like bathrooms. I would bring in really pretty, simple textiles—often a bath mat, towels, and a shower curtain—all within a unified color palette that I knew the owner loved. The addition of a few basic items such as cool storage containers and pretty vessels, a candle, and some greenery can make a huge difference. It typically took no more than an afternoon to add beauty and interest to that once-dated space. When our clients saw the look of their "new" bathroom, they never seemed to notice their old, outdated tile. The key to this was diverting their attention from what they didn't love to all that was new and beautiful.

It's those types of projects that have been the most gratifying for me as a designer. Not only had I fulfilled a promise to our clients, but they were also able to see that it's possible to update even the most drab spaces into something that they could love—not next year, or even next month—but *now*.

Very few people actually get to build their homes from the studs up, exactly the way they want and tailored to their specific needs. Most of us are just working with what we've got. When we moved into the farmhouse, each room came with a pretty rigid footprint because of the old bones of the home. On top of that, we had a tight budget.

My goal in each space was to create a simple and attractive backdrop with modest materials. I chose inexpensive tile with a timeless quality that I knew I could happily live with for the foreseeable future. It was simple white with octagonal dots, and, similar to the rest of the materials we chose for the bathrooms, it was in a clean, neutral palette. Over time, I layered in good-quality textiles and small but intentional design details to give it the elevated look I wanted. Perhaps if we had had a more generous budget I would have chosen nicer materials or something a little more unique for the tile, but having kept the foundation as simple as I did has created a lot of margin for creativity over the years. It has given me the opportunity to easily incorporate new elements or change out textiles whenever I felt like updating the look of these spaces.

Bathrooms can be a pretty common pain point in a lot of houses because they typically have to work for a range of people every single day. I like to start the design process of any bathroom remodel with a clear understanding of who will be using it. I use this approach whether a home has one or multiple bathrooms.

In the previous chapter, I talked about creating a retreat in the master bedroom. I like to consider the master bathroom an extension of that retreat. So I don't take this space lightly. I tend to be equally intentional about design as I am about function in the master bathroom. Ample storage is essential here. I think that when this space is well thought out and organized, it can become that helping hand you're grateful for during those early morning moments standing before the mirror looking for the dental floss. When I consider how I want a master bath to look and feel, I always start by pulling some inspiration—perhaps a wall color or a similar piece of art—from the master bedroom to create a sense of cohesiveness among these separate spaces.

The kids' bathroom is one of the most hardworking spaces in the home. Whether you have one child or five utilizing it, the biggest challenge is making each kid feel like it's theirs, in both function and personality. In my own house, I've found that labeled drawers and assigned towel hooks help keep this space tidy. Historically, if I don't give my kids a place for their toothbrush and towel, somehow both end up on the floor. When I first incorporated these simple design safeguards into my kids' bathroom, they reacted as though I'd just unloaded a bag of new, shiny toys—and almost immediately they showed a sense of ownership over their small portion of this shared room.

It can be easy to focus all our efforts on the functionality of a room like this, and I can see the value of function over form in a bathroom for kids, or even adults, but a home's atmosphere—no matter the room—should always reflect conscious choices if they really are to say something about who we are and what we value.

That's what I love most about the powder room. If it isn't serving as a primary bathroom, this is a room where design can often have free rein. Typically, this space isn't highly functional, so everything—the mirror, the hardware, the towels, and the art—can be interesting or beautiful. Tile and wallpaper choices are a good way to infuse a little something that you love. This is a great place to not take ourselves too seriously. (So, if you happen to really love peacocks, put up some peacock wallpaper!) The powder room might also be the most frequently used public space in our homes, especially if you like to have guests over. Hospitality is knitted into nearly everything I'm passionate about, which makes designing a powder room a really fun undertaking for me.

If a major renovation isn't in the cards for the bathroom in your home, consider modest changes you can make that will elevate this space to a place that you love, and will help to stave off the urge for a more major overhaul until the time is right. If it's the finishes that feel old and outdated, switch out the hardware for something more timeless. Layering in pretty textiles, like a bath mat, towels, and a shower curtain, is a simple and affordable way to add beauty to a space like this and, in my experience, can work great in distracting attention away from any unloved materials or finishes.

This book really isn't about spending a fortune and having everything you want. That's certainly not what I hope you take away from these pages. Rather, to me, the joy in design is the challenge and gratification of creating a space that *feels* like home every moment that you spend within its walls. When it comes to the bathroom, that means envisioning how to best support the daily patterns of the ones we live with, and creating an environment that reflects those. This thoughtful approach can help everyone put their best foot forward day in and day out. It typically takes no more than a few thoughtful additions to make even a hardworking space like the bathroom feel like home.

(*Page 206*) This guest bathroom was originally part of the unfinished attic when we moved in, so I had a pretty unique footprint to work with, including the pitched roof. We installed a sink into an antique dresser, which adds a bit of character to this clean and simple space. The white subway tile is timeless and keeps the overall look of this room feeling bright and clean. (*Page 208*) The antique doors and frame make for a grand entrance into our master bathroom, so I kept the rest of the materials simple and polished. This has allowed the textiles in here to be the statement-makers. The hanging chandelier matches the one in our bedroom, which connects these two spaces and adds some charm to the bathroom. (*Above*) Our small powder room felt like the perfect spot to incorporate this classic black and white striped wallpaper. I'd had this vintage mirror for a while, and I love the drama it adds to this small space.

BATHROOMS: WHAT TO CONSIDER

Bathrooms can be expensive to remodel and impossible to ignore. But it doesn't take much to improve these small spaces, no matter what you're working with today. In this chapter there are a lot of beautiful examples that I think will serve as inspiration for your own spaces, and equip you to create bathrooms that are both beautiful and functional.

PRACTICAL PIECES

- Good lighting and storage top the list of practical elements to consider in a bathroom. Take note how spaces in this chapter utilize both.

PLAY IT UP

- When it comes to selecting materials that will define the aesthetic of your bathroom, I typically suggest timeless options that are in keeping with the style and architecture of your home. However, as many of the spaces in this chapter suggest, I also love when clients choose to play up these spaces by adding unique, personalized details that are fun and interesting for guests. These smaller rooms are the best spots to try bolder design ideas.

- Consider the stylistic details that are resonating with you. If you have high ceilings, you can emphasize that height with a more dramatic light fixture. You can also incorporate a vintage mirror to add some charm. And if there's room for a tub, by all means, get a tub!

THE ELEMENTS

- NEW BATH MAT AND TOWELS
- CATCHALL TRAY
- HOOKS
- SHELVING OR STORAGE
- VANITY LIGHT

- OVERSIZE MIRROR
- AMPLE COUNTER SPACE
- BASKETS OR BINS
- TOWEL HOOKS
- SHOWER CURTAIN

In the master bathroom at Hillcrest Estate, I wanted to incorporate details that would make it feel warm and inviting. I chose simple Shaker cabinets for the vanity and painted them a rich gray, and the walls a soft white for contrast. The beautiful marble accents on the floor and vanity tie the grays and the whites together, while the brass accents represent a modern interpretation of a classic look that's well-suited to this historic house.

The custom vanity in this master bathroom provides so much flexible storage, making this space extremely functional. I balanced the clean lines of the black hexagonal floor tiles with a warm stain for the vanity. A way that I personalized this space was by placing a saying that is significant to the homeowners in a spot where I knew they could see the words every day.

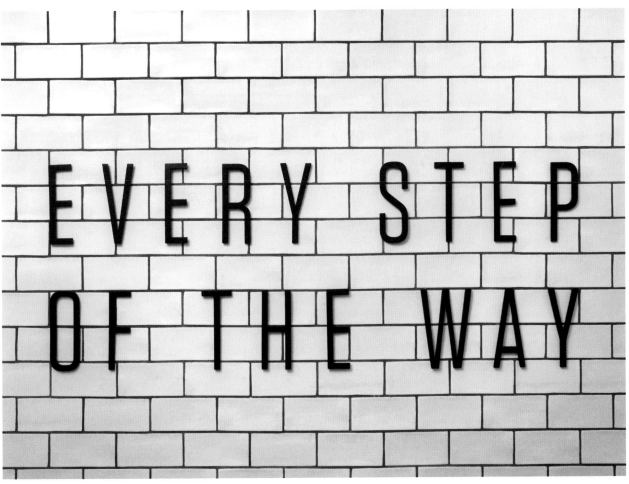

This bathroom was designed for a teenage boy. I incorporated a darker marble than I typically use to create a more masculine look. The white plantation shutters offer privacy and also provide a light contrast to the moodier colors that fill this space. The bold floor tile brings in a fun and youthful element.

The industrial lines in this master bathroom, mixed with the organic feel of the Saltillo tile and white oak cabinets, make for an unexpected yet attractive pairing. Rather than choosing a typical cabinet to go above the toilet, I added metal and glass open shelving that matches the style of the gridded glass of the walk-in steam shower. A small teak bench adds some style and serves as an additional surface.

This master bathroom feels like a spa retreat. The teak wood, paired with the sleek glass, makes this walk-in shower the focal feature. Creamy white walls, warm cabinetry, and clean-lined mirrors help make the design of this long, narrow room feel tranquil yet super intentional. Hooks are an attractive and efficient way to display and dry towels.

These homeowners did an amazing job at creating a space that truly feels one of a kind. From the wallpaper to the bold, black-painted vanity and small marble tulip side table, this bathroom boasts a unique style that feels both eclectic and timeless. A cloudscape wallpaper print wraps the walls and ceiling for an added sense of whimsy.

This home has a layered and eclectic style. I didn't want each room to compete or feel too overpowering, so I kept this hall bathroom a little more simple and clean, primarily using black and white materials for the shower, flooring, countertops, walls, and hardware. To add some drama, I chose a bold color for the cabinets and an oversize custom mirror to elevate the aesthetic of this space and to suit the overall vibe of the home. If there's a particular light feature that you love, consider using it in an unconventional way. These two pendants flanking the mirror are a fun alternative to typical decorative vanity fixtures.

Because this guest bathroom is right off a more masculine-styled bedroom in Hillcrest Estate, I wanted to carry that look into this space as well. To offset the darker accents, I incorporated white shiplap walls and a marble countertop to help lighten it up. To give this room a fun, finishing touch, I chose this plaid-patterned tile, which feels both classic and modern. This tile was pricey, but because the footprint of this space is small, I didn't have to spend a lot for it to make an impact.

The square footage of this guest bathroom is small, but the homeowners have really max-imized the space they have. The three-tiered recessed shelving above the toilet makes use of empty wall space for much-needed storage. The homeowners chose to play with scale in this inset shelf, which makes for added interest. Instead of tearing down walls and building out a more traditionally shaped room, these homeowners chose to transform this architectural quirk into a design statement that is also functional for the people who use this space every day. The floating farmhouse sink not only serves as a unique fo-cal point, but also keeps the room feeling uncluttered and frees up valuable floor space where a woven basket stands in for additional storage. Floor-to-ceiling tile makes for a cool, practical design detail.

The attention to detail in this guest bathroom does not go unnoticed. The existing primitive materials of the home, such as the shutters, trim, and wide-planked floors, provide the perfect backdrop for the high contrast of black and white used throughout this space. An industrial stool offers an unexpected surface, while the makeshift antique vanity provides a place for getting ready.

The color-blocked tiled wall (*above*) was a splurge, but the homeowers loved the added layer of personality, so I made it the focal point of their bathroom by keeping the rest of the space clean and simple. The teal hue of the tile and the teak-wood vanity are both elements that are used throughout the home. One of my favorite pieces in this space is the custom white metal shelf that hangs above the bathtub. It's functional but also makes a unique design element—almost serving as a piece of art against the tiled accent wall. You can always search for a local craftsman willing to work with you to create a custom piece. Some of my most-loved design elements, like this one, have come from swapping ideas with those who are experts in their field.

This guest bathroom features an industrial aesthetic with simple, timeless design elements. Since it's a small room with a black-and-white color palette, I played up the texture with three different types of tile. I chose a black hexagon tile for the main floor, a small white octagonal pattern for the shower floor, and then classic subway tile for the shower walls. If you are sticking with a limited color palette, mix up your material choices to highlight interesting shapes and textures. The metal light fixture, clean-lined mirror, and concrete countertop help to define this space in a modern, industrial style. I added in a small potted plant and textured towels to help soften all the hard lines in this bathroom.

(*Above*) If you don't like the look of open shelving, glass cabinets are a beautiful, more traditional option for bathroom storage. Toiletries can easily be kept out of sight in baskets or closed storage and folded towels can be stacked on shelves for a clean, organized look, keeping the vanity free of unnecessary clutter. (*Opposite*) The personalized tile in this bathroom entry offers a cheerful welcome to anyone who enters. This room has a refined traditional aesthetic, which is made personal with the playful tile. Look for any areas of unused space in your bathrooms and consider adding a vanity area, bench, or additional storage.

Tall, thin custom mirrors flank the window in this master bathroom, giving the illusion of a larger space. The custom midcentury walnut vanity and modern black hardware represent the homeowners' style, while also nodding to the home's original Craftsman-era features, with a classic subway tile backsplash and marble hexagonal flooring. Natural light is exceedingly valuable in any room, but in a bathroom, it's critical. Consider installing new or larger windows to allow in as much light as possible.

TROUBLESHOOTING

OUTDATED CABINETRY

In older homes, the bathroom cabinets are typically a lot lower than what you see in newer homes. Replacing vanities allows you to raise the height for a more updated look. We typically do 34" to 36" finished height vanities (with countertop). If you can't switch out your cabinets, consider a fresh coat of paint or simply update the hardware.

INSUFFICIENT STORAGE

A few great storage solutions for the bathroom include over-the-toilet storage, ladders to hang towels, shelving units, and baskets. Consider adding open shelves or maximizing hidden storage with bins and baskets to keep clutter off the counters. Vanity trays can help keep products you prefer to display looking tidy and organized. If space allows, install a medicine cabinet to help accommodate small toiletries.

NEED FOR NATURAL LIGHT VS. NEED FOR PRIVACY

Windows keep the natural light coming in, but in order to keep this space private, consider a frosted glass option. You can also add a window treatment like roman shades or plantation shutters for a more styled look.

DINGY TILE OR TUB

If you're ready to make a dramatic change, replacing old tile can certainly transform the look of your bathroom. However, you can have it reglazed or refinished instead for a fresh look. You can also keep it simple by updating your linens and accessories to play off of the existing tile colors, which can help them blend in better.

SPACE IS TIGHT

If you're looking for more square footage, consider converting your tub to a standing shower stall or changing a sink vanity from a cabinet to a pedestal. This will reduce the amount of storage you have, but if storage isn't an issue, a pedestal sink will open up the room and give you additional floor space. Decorative wall shelves are another nice solution for extra storage. Make sure you also have ample lighting, and select an oversize mirror that will give the illusion of more space.

CHAPTER

08

KID SPACES

When our remodeling company was just starting to gain traction, Chip and I were doing all sorts of renovation projects, including some beautiful old properties in a historic part of Waco called Castle Heights. It's full of stately old homes with well-kept lawns and established trees. It all seemed so far out of reach for Chip and me, and yet once we started working in those homes, I began to dream about living there ourselves. I truly thought it would take years of saving for us to get a house there, but it wasn't long before Chip stumbled upon an opportunity to buy a gorgeous 1920s Tudor-style house right in the heart of that idyllic neighborhood.

We began renovations and shortly after we'd finished, we were asked if our house could be featured in some regional magazines. We couldn't believe it. All that attention somehow led to me putting a ton of pressure on myself to always have my home looking spotless and beautiful. I'm not exactly sure what the logic was there, and I may not have been able to see it then, but I felt like it was suddenly my job to maintain a perfect home. With four young kids, this was no small feat. I found that as my children were getting older, it became nearly impossible for me to maintain both a picture-perfect home and a practical, usable space for my family. I would spend most of the day following my kids around, picking up piles of building blocks and books, sometimes before they were even done with them. One afternoon, in a state of exhaustion, I realized that something just wasn't right. I looked around and saw a lot of "perfection" and thought, *But where do my kids hang out? Why don't they have anywhere to really play in this house?* Suddenly, it hit me. In my nonstop efforts to make the house look good for a bunch of anonymous strangers, I had failed to create a space where my children could simply be kids.

Around that same time, Chip came home and announced that he'd found a couple who wanted to buy our Castle Heights house, so he'd gone out and put an offer on a new house that we would flip and then move into. I'd just had this epiphany about making our home more functional for our entire family, but surely that didn't mean I had to move out of my dream house. Chip didn't hesitate to remind me that this house was never meant to be forever. Flipping that house was how we put food on the table. It was our livelihood. We'd both agreed on this lifestyle years before, but with each house we flipped, I grew more attached to the home we'd created. I couldn't see it then, but I think Chip knew there was something better waiting for us just a little further down the road.

① supplies
② practice strokes
③ alphabet
④ go for it!

N. 4TH ST.

The next day Chip took me to see the house he was hoping to purchase. It was a long, one-story gray house that had been built in the 1980s. It had *no* character and *no* charm. The bland look of this house didn't make me feel any better about having to leave our gorgeous Tudor-style home, but I got on board, pumping myself up for all that a new season with a fresh perspective might hold. There was a part of me that felt motivated by the challenge to create beauty in a house that seemed to have so little potential.

Beyond that, I felt like this new house, unwanted as it was, just might be the do-over I needed to really be able to prioritize my family in the design of our home. That was my first-

ever truly intentional design goal: I wanted to make every house we would ever live in be for and about us.

I wasn't sure how I'd actually make this happen until I took the kids over to that drab shotgun house one day to start sketching out some remodeling ideas. The front door was at one end and the house just shot back from there in this long, straight, narrow rectangle, with a hallway that ran the length of the house. Just as quickly as I opened the door the kids took off down that hall, giggling and squealing. I hadn't done a thing to that house yet, and already my kids were having a better time in it than I'd ever seen them have in our big, beautiful house in Castle Heights.

That's when I had an epiphany that started to change absolutely everything for me. My kids loved it in this house. They could be kids. I decided right then and there that I would design everything with that in mind. There were two good-size living rooms in the house, and I was determined to figure out how I could make one of them specifically for our children. I felt determined to find a way to make it both practical for my kids and aesthetically pleasing to Chip and me. With fresh eyes, I began to look at both rooms and how I could fill them. I had this long wooden candle holder, into which, in past homes, I'd placed tall votives in each of its twelve holes. This time I filled it with colorful crayons and placed it as the centerpiece of the kids' craft table. All of a sudden, it became this design element that I loved, and it was providing something functional for my kids.

Over the next few months, I watched my kids come alive. I'm telling you, I couldn't pull them out of that room. For the first time, I saw how inspiring it was for them when I simply carved out a space that could stretch their young imaginations. I realized that as parents we can either lose our minds to our kids' messes and the endless cleanups or we can choose another perspective. It was important to me that I create a home that invites my kids to be a central part of it, and that communicates not only to our family but also to any guest who enters that this home is for *all* of us. The years we lived in the shotgun house were when I learned the value in this kind of design—one that serves the people who actually live in a home more than anyone who may just be looking in. Seeing my family thrive became infinitely more motivating than keeping up with the Joneses ever was. Those same ideals continue to influence my design choices to this day, whether for a client or for our own family.

Spaces we've designated for our kids have looked different in every house we've lived in. When the kids were all pretty young, Chip built a kid-size farmhouse table that we placed in our kitchen, only because there really was no other practical place to put it. I kept it well stocked with art supplies and educational tools—anything that encouraged them to learn or to create. I loved seeing them busy at that table. Sometimes I thought it was a little bit magical how well it occupied their young, curious minds.

Whether it's a table like the one Chip built, a compact built-in desk with a low chair, or a fully functioning playroom, kids feel valued when there's a place at home created just for them. At the farm, we converted the unfinished attic into livable square footage. It's ideal for kids because of the many nooks and crannies that we've carved out as different types of spots for them—like a coffee bar where they can sit and do their homework, a table that's designated for painting and drawing, and a playful desk and small library for reading a good book.

One thing that has become an evolving lesson for me is how to create a space that actually inspires my kids. I've learned how to become a student of them, to really get on their level and meet them where they're at. I've watched my kids seek out nooks and secret hideouts, relishing the feeling of being on an adventure. Many of these observations have encouraged me to alter some of my own design preferences when I'm creating a space that's for them. I tend to opt for uncluttered simplicity in my home, keeping most things hidden away. But I've happily chosen to give some of that up for the sake of my kids' creativity. My priority is to unapologetically make spaces for my kids to be kids, even when it needs to be in a shared living space.

If you are willing to flip the script on what a home *should* look like and instead focus on designing it around and for the people who live in it, the entire feel and intention of your house will change for the better. Typically, the most challenging part is embracing the idea that your house will look different from everybody else's. That, by the way, is a really, really good thing. If it's telling your family's story, then it will be uniquely yours. From that point, it's a scavenger hunt of finding items that look good in your space but that also serve a practical purpose for the kids. I've found that I can repurpose pieces like crayons or Legos into playful art by stashing them in attractive canisters. This is the easiest way to embrace them being visible on a shelf or table so the kids feel encouraged to play.

One of my favorite renovations I've ever done was for clients with triplets. The couple had gone from just the two of them living in a house to sharing it with three babies. Overnight,

it seemed, their three kids were toddling around, and pretty quickly they realized their house was not working for them anymore. They found themselves in the same place I had been in the day I felt that wave of regret that there was no place in my house for my kids to really be themselves. Our clients were willing to toss out the status quo and convert their formal dining room into a full-blown kids' playroom. This space happened to be the first room guests passed when they walked into the house, but our clients didn't mind. In fact, they embraced the statement it was making to anyone who came over. This season of their life was all about their kids, and their home reflected that. What I love most about the choice they made was that it actually cost them something emotionally. They didn't have a spare room just waiting for a purpose. Their dining room certainly had a clear purpose already, and I'm sure it was tough at times not to have that useful space during the years their children occupied it.

Still, I think they would agree that very little beats having a house that meets the needs of the stage of life that you're actually in. There's a good chance that a few years down the road, when their kids are grown, they'll convert that space back to a dining room. They'll be able to seat their kids' friends and growing families around their dinner table. But that time isn't yet.

That's what's so beautiful about the rooms that fill our homes. They each have a journey of their own. Some years they're functioning in one way only to be changed later for a more pressing purpose. They're there to be molded and shaped to become what we most deeply need them to be.

In whatever season you find yourself today, consider how you can make your house meaningful for each person who calls it home.

(*Page 242*) My kids love to paint and draw at this schoolhouse-style craft table. Small floating shelves make getting paints and brushes easy while an antique sugar mold holds crayons and colored pencils. (*Page 244*) This vintage wooden chicken coop is being re-purposed here as toy storage. The kids love to grab-and-go from this spot. The large chalkboard encourages creativity and the hanging swing (*page 245*) makes for a fun, playful addition to this attic play space. (*Page 247*) An antique floating shelf and vintage barstools create a fun little coffee bar. My kids love to pretend that they're at a coffee shop when they're doing homework, so this is one of their favorite spots. (*Above*) This playful desk and small library is where my kids can do homework or read a good book in a spot that's all their own.

CRITICAL
THINKING
IN DESIGN

KID SPACES:
WHAT TO CONSIDER

One of the most difficult aspects of designing a kids' space is determining what style will easily age with them, as well as how to create something that's exciting and fun, but still looks and feels consistent with the rest of the home. I don't think it's lost on our children when they see that we've made the effort to create a space just for them.

MAKE IT PERSONAL, MAKE IT LAST

- Take note of how these different areas incorporate unique personalizations and functional elements that encourage both creativity and organization.

- Notice how the bedroom styles in this chapter are executed. Rather than focusing on literal interpretations of a theme, decor and furnishings are incorporated in a way that will age with the children.

- Determine how these spaces are being defined within the larger context of the home.

- In what ways are small or large rooms being repurposed to serve these homeowners' seasons of life? Consider the elements and details in each space that you can utilize in your own home.

THE ELEMENTS

- COLOR AND PATTERNS
- ORGANIZATIONAL BASKETS
- BOOKSHELF
- STEP STOOL
- BLACKBOARD

- BUNK BEDS
- READING NOOK
- PERSONAL KEEPSAKES
- DESK LIGHT
- TOY TRUNK

I wanted the character of my girls' bedroom to match their personalities. I chose architectural elements that are whimsical and fun, like the chandelier, canopy bed, and hanging nightstands, while the feminine colors and ornate details of the bedding embody a soft side, just like Ella and Emmie Kay. Dimensional pieces, like this antique mantel that doubles as a blackboard (*above*), make for playful design statements in a kids' room. I like my kids to feel that they're part of the design process so that they have a sense of ownership in their room. My girls both love the color blue, so we did a soft shade with gray undertones on the walls that acts as a neutral and pairs well with any color.

My boys love adventure, and I wanted their room to reflect that. They practically live outside, so I pulled in some outdoor elements like the galvanized awnings above their windows and a turf area rug. The boys have friends and cousins over a lot, so we built bunk beds with the inevitable sleepover in mind. For as long as I can remember, the boys have loved Legos and all sorts of games, but they tend to get left all over the floor of their bedroom. For this reason, I incorporated a ton of storage space in the form of a dresser, a desk outfitted with labeled boxes, caddies hung on the wall, and under-bed wicker baskets, so that at the end of the day, everything has a proper place. To make their space feel personal to them, each boy has a desk that's all his own. I also added a few pieces that hold significance, like the number 16 pillow (*above*), which was once Chip's baseball number and now is both Drake's and Duke's as well.

In this bedroom, I wanted to create a space that looked great while still being kid-friendly, fun, and functional for the boys who use it every day. The raw skinnylap walls used throughout pair well with the black metal accents, like the window awning (*pages 254–255*), desk chair, and railing.

When it comes to a bedroom shared by sisters, it's fun to consider creative ways to reflect the things that inspire each of them. In this bedroom, I highlighted one side of the room with a bold yet playful wallpaper, and then kept everything else simple with subtle hints of pink to complement the accent wall.

This design is a great example of maximizing the space you have to work with. This room is small in size and unique in shape, yet these homeowners were able to fit three twin beds in here. I love the way they got creative in this room. The headboards double as storage cubbies, giving each kid a space of his own. This is an easy project that makes for an extremely efficient and usable design element, not to mention it's just plain cool.

I had so much fun dreaming of ways I could make this wall come alive for our clients' sons who were born with a rare genetic condition that requires them to rely on wheelchairs for their mobility. My goal in this space was to create a functional room that would encourage independence and creativity for these boys. The toys and books needed to be wheelchair accessible, so we incorporated hanging caddies and a bookshelf to be within arm's reach. The personalized details in here are my favorite. Marquee letters make for a fun display that can easily change to reflect their current season of life. The look on the two boys' faces when they saw their names above their beds was a moment I won't forget.

(*Opposite*) It was important to these homeowners to have a room in their house where their grandchildren could play. They had a spare bedroom, and gave me free rein to design something fun and unique. I loved creating this nontraditional, whimsical play space. (*Above*) In an effort to make this second-story landing more than just a wall that you dead-end into, I added recessed shelving that could function as a great spot for books and baskets of toys. I love the old hardware sign and the unconventional character it brings to this small space.

This work/play space is in a very visible part of the home—it's almost an extension of the den—so it has been designed to blend seamlessly with the rest of the room by using like colors. The classroom-style chairs and abundance of counter space provide the kids with plenty of room to create.

This second-story living room is used as a casual family space. It adjoins the kids' playroom so it's often utilized as a place for continued play or to rest and relax. The paper airplane art above the sofa and the assortment of collected antiques make the space feel more playful than the more formal living room downstairs.

These boys love camping and being outdoors, so I chose this mountain landscape wallpaper *(pages 270–271 and opposite)* as the backdrop behind their beds so they could get the sense that every day is an adventure. I added additional texture to this space with the bedding, in colors and patterns the boys love. It's valuable for kids to be able to personalize their rooms, but it can help to create some parameters, so I incorporated a wire wall display where they can post their favorite photos, notes, and mementos all in one place.

When Chip and I purchased this historic house in Waco, there was a small structure at the back of the property that looked like it could be an ideal kids' playhouse. When we decided to flip the main house and turn it into a vacation rental, I gave this cottage a makeover for the little ones to enjoy when they visited.

My girls love to help me in the kitchen, especially if it means they get to wear an apron, so I designed this dreamy kid-size space similar to how I might plan any grown-up kitchen. I incorporated a few of my favorite things like concrete countertops, open shelving, organizational baskets, and a farmhouse table for eating. It's hard to admit, but I like it a tiny bit more than my own kitchen.

These homeowners wanted to create a fun and adventurous space for their grandkids, who enjoy playing on the monkey bars and taking a ride down the slide that sits beside the stairwell. There seems to be something unexpected in every corner of this bedroom, where a limited use of bright shades of color add a playfulness to the overall style.

All that this homeowner's daughter wanted was a rainbow room. Rather than taking that literally, I softened the typical rainbow color palette with a paint-washed ombre accent wall in multiple shades of pink, blue, and yellow. The same color palette is repeated in the macramé wall hanging on the adjacent wall. I incorporated a hanging rattan chair to play up the Bohemian style of the bedroom and to give this little girl a comfortable place to relax or read.

TROUBLESHOOTING

LET KIDS BE A PART OF THE PROCESS

When planning a kids' space, narrow down the choices to a few options that you genuinely like and think your kids will love. Do the editing first and then involve them in the final choices to help guide the process and keep the overall look cohesive.

AVOIDING CLUTTER

Install built-in cabinets with lots of drawers or simply include baskets and furniture with built-in storage where toys and items can be hidden away. Using labels on bins or baskets will help everyone know what goes where when it's time for cleanup.

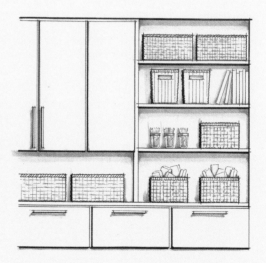

TOYS EVERYWHERE

Designate places in your home just for your children. When my kids were little, I remember putting toys in one of the bottom drawers of our kitchen so they could play while I would cook. Look for other creative ways to incorporate a few of their favorite things in main living spaces, perhaps by storing toys, books, or games in a piece of furniture or in a basket that blends into the style of the room.

MAINTAINING A SENSE
OF DESIGN IN A KID SPACE

Thoughtfully select where you want to include pattern and color in a space. Sometimes, fun wallpaper or a paint color can do the trick, and then you can keep the furniture and bedding in neutral shades. Or, you can do the reverse and have a more neutral wall and incorporate color with the bedding, pillows, and artwork. You can also keep it simple and let the toys and books be the added color. In kids' rooms, as much as anywhere else, editing is key. Don't feel like you have to fill every empty space. Just like adults, kids can feel scattered and overwhelmed if their spaces are cluttered.

SMALL FOOTPRINT
FOR SHARED ROOMS

Bunk beds are the ultimate solution for fitting more than one bed in a small room, while lofted beds can also help to create additional space for a desk or reading nook. Trundle beds can provide more sleeping possibilities while also freeing up precious square footage during the day. If none of these solutions is an option, consider moving toys and playthings to a den or playroom and reserving the bedroom for sleeping and dressing.

ROOMS THAT ARE
QUICKLY OUTGROWN

Instead of being overly literal with themes in your children's spaces, choose decorative elements and concepts in a consistent color palette that are broader and less specific. These choices are more likely to remain relevant and age appropriate as your child matures, allowing the room design to last longer. Instead of a theme, a room filled with thoughtful details can make it feel playful and imaginative rather than forced.

ROOMS TO RETREAT

Before we begin demo on a client's house, I have this tradition of doing an initial walk-through of the entire property, just as it is. I like to go by myself, to learn what I can about the life and memories its storied walls hold. I wait to take this little tour until after we've had several planning meetings with the new owners of the home. This allows me to move from room to room, thinking about the owners' specific story and needs. I love to spend this extra time looking for opportunities where I can surprise them with an additional place that will inspire them on a daily basis. So I like to leave a little margin in my design plan for this walk-through and the potential of what else could be.

I really believe that every nook and cranny of our homes should be working hard to meet our needs as well as our interests. These walk-throughs allow me the time and space to look for any unaccounted-for areas that I can creatively give new purpose to. I like to look with fresh eyes at a spare closet or dead space beneath a staircase. Then I tend to imagine a built-in desk in that mostly unused closet or a little reading nook tucked beneath the stairs. If you can begin to examine your own home through the lens of untapped potential, I think you'll be surprised by what you find.

I *love* a well-used home. The maximizer in me can't wait to create something valuable where there once was only wasted space. Only in the last decade have I tapped into using this extra square footage in a way that truly gives the most bang for the buck, and not necessarily in the sense of a traditional investment or resale strategy. Rather, this is more about making room for the things that fill us up, inspire us, or help us pursue a goal or dream.

For a while, I led my life with the notion that I could do everything and be everything, at work and at home, without falling short somewhere along the way. It wasn't that I was trying to impress anybody—I genuinely wanted to have my hand in all aspects of the everyday operation of our business and also never miss a family moment. I kept up this juggling act as long as I could without ever really pausing to refuel myself. Not surprisingly, it eventually caught up with me. I started to get frustrated by small, everyday things and I found myself lacking the energy to pursue what I actually cared about most. It was in one of our early homes, which we called the shotgun house because of the way it shot straight back on our property, that I remember first really pausing intentionally. In that moment, I began to see that when life starts to spin out of control, it's time to go back to the fundamental things that ground me. In that season of life, all of our kids were still pretty young and I spent the majority of my day at home with them. I realized then that I didn't have to be involved in every aspect of our business, so for the first time in a long time, I said no to some things and delegated some others. I had recently started to really focus on creating spaces for my kids where they could actually be kids, messy floors and all, and I realized that I, too, needed a place to be inspired. I decided to be as intentional about making a space for myself as I had been in creating one for them. Our house didn't have a backyard to work with and less square footage than the house we'd just left, but there was just enough land on the side of the house to fence in and turn into our very first garden. Because we were limited in space, the garden was small, but I savored every inch of it. Whenever I felt that tug to refuel, I'd head out there and spend some time tending to my plants. There was something about messing with the soil and caring for their growth that reminded me that my own life is a gift and that it cannot flourish unless it is well tended.

I suppose I could have toughed it out in that house and just gotten by, knowing that because of how often Chip was having us move, we'd be on to the next place soon enough. Was creating a space for myself worth the trouble? But instead of hanging on to the idea of what the future might hold, I intentionally created that little garden to be everything I needed it to be for me right then. Today, I have a beautiful and useful garden shed beyond what I could have dreamed of back then, filled with inspiration for what my work and life need from me, but no more so than that little patch of garden did all those years ago. And the same goes for the other retreats I've carved out for myself or for my family during the time in between. They were each just right for what that season of life required. Before there was a garden shed, I had an outdoor garden at the farm where I'd retreat in moments when I felt like I was running on empty. Before that, it was, quite honestly, my laundry room, never to actually start a load, but to simply sit with a cup of coffee and the scent of my favorite candle. And long before that, it was that small, fenced-in wooden square on the side of the shotgun house. These spaces have taken different forms and sizes, but they've all served me equally well as the one place where I can really feel the stresses of the day begin to fall away.

I imagine I'm not alone in this. Perhaps you, too, can recognize when it's time to seek a place where you can refuel and feel made anew to do the things you care about, well and with your whole self. That is what this chapter is all about.

Having a place to retreat to may seem like a luxury, but it doesn't have to be. In some of the houses I've lived in, this place for me has simply been an oversize chair in the corner of a room. Still, these areas have become so restorative for me in my own home that they're something I want for everyone. No small part of my design strategy in each and every project I work on is making sure that this concept is built in. I think it's that important. You may already lovingly refer to a space as the "reading corner" or the "craft room" and that's exactly what I love about them. They will be fundamentally different in each of our homes because they are intended to be made distinctly unique for each of us. They can facilitate something you love, like journaling or crafts, or support a need that your family may have in this season, such as a work-from-home desk built into a small office nook. It can even look as simple as a hammock strung between two trees where you can enjoy your coffee without interruption. With a little creative reimagining, these spaces can actually be pretty simple to carve out.

What often ends up stalling these projects is a resistance to the idea of changing a room from what may be its originally intended function. If that feeling resonates with you on any level, it's time to lose those expectations. When you allow yourself to think first about the needs of your own family rather than some theoretical floor plan, you will begin to fall more in love with the home that you're in as it will finally be on its way to functioning as you need it to. Perhaps your garage could more usefully function as a workout room or that formal dining room would better serve your family as a playroom for the kids. Why not transform these rooms into something that better reflects the people who live there and the season of life that they are actually in?

When I've repurposed a space for a client in this way, they are typically surprised by how often they find themselves retreating to this place more than anywhere else in the house. Each day they head back to this room to pick up where they left off the day before on whatever the project might be. More than the larger, more impressive rooms they may have dreamed of for so long, they find that this ends up being the place they never want to leave.

(*Page 284*) I designed this shed to be a practical resource within the large garden. It's also a place where our family can go to work on creative projects, or for gathering and entertaining. Antique pendants and a raw-stone fireplace elevate the room and add a sophisticated tone to this rustic space. (*Page 287*) Since this shed also facilitates work in the garden, I wanted it to be not only inspiring but also hardworking. This boot rack makes our everyday tools more accessible. (*Above*) I love plants and antique books, so I filled this wall of open shelving with old gardening books and some of my favorite potted plants.

CRITICAL
THINKING
IN DESIGN

ROOMS TO RETREAT: WHAT TO CONSIDER

The rooms we're featuring in this chapter are varied and may look nothing like the space you have to work with in your own home, but my hope is that you can tune in to certain elements you feel drawn to and let those inspire whatever space you long to create.

CONSIDER YOUR SEASON OF LIFE

- Could you use a place for your kids to practice their instruments after school? Would it be amazing to have a reading or writing nook for you or your spouse to unwind in at the end of the day? Or is there a need that could easily be solved with a little extra space, perhaps a creative studio space or a simple desk area for those work-from-home days?

MAXIMIZE SPACE

- If you'd really love an office but what you have is a single wall or a corner, take a look at how some of these homeowners have created a work area using only an empty wall, floating shelf, and reading lamp, and called it good.

- Look around for any unused space in your own home that you can creatively repurpose.

THE ELEMENTS

- INSPIRING DECOR
- COMFORTABLE SEATING
- SHELVING OR STORAGE
- ARTIST'S EASEL
- BOOKSHELF

- TOOLS OF THE TRADE
- SCENTED CANDLE
- TASK LIGHTING
- JOURNAL OR PLANNER
- MUSIC PLAYER AND SPEAKERS

While this is the room where I do my family's laundry, I wanted to make it more purposeful than just that one function—not to mention more enjoyable to spend time in while I wash and fold. So I mixed in my collections of plants and cake stands, as well as some framed art and a favorite-scented candle. Now it's a place that makes me happy even when I'm doing chores—or when I'm not.

(*Above*) The square footage of this house is pretty small, so I wanted to be thoughtful about how I was designing every last inch of the space these homeowners had. This bright corner of their living room provided just enough space for a piece of furniture. Rather than filling it with something that wouldn't have provided much function, I placed a writing desk here, making it an ideal spot for thoughtful reflection or a quiet retreat. The vintage leather wingback chair reflects this couple's love for pieces with character and history, while the raw-edge desk brings a modern shape and rustic material to the space. (*Left*) Attics are common in older houses, and at the time they were being built, they really weren't meant to be seen. In the spirit of utilizing every inch of house available to us, Chip and I chose to make this space at our farmhouse one that could offer something to everyone in our family. Our shared craft room is where we can all go to create. I like to use this space any time I get the urge to do something a little more hands-on creatively. I've also had a few friends over for a low-key craft night.

Storage and organization are prioritized in this workroom in a way that highlights items the homeowners love. They've found a way to make this room utilitarian as well as in-spiring. The open bookshelf provides texture and color to this space through the objects that are on display. Here, the books and plants become colorful art, since the rest of the space is pretty neutral.

This spot is for game lovers and puzzlers. It also makes for a great place to read or have conversations. Even though this space is set apart as a game room, I also wanted it to feel connected to the rest of the house. I incorporated antique finishes and decor pieces, such as a large vintage map and art prints, to blend in with the style of this historic home.

TROUBLESHOOTING

UNINSPIRED

Start by figuring out what you need. Is it an office, a craft room, or maybe a reading nook? Then, determine what kind of space could serve that purpose well. Once the focus of the space is sorted out, begin to feel inspired about how you want to fill it to make it a place that you love. If you're lacking inspiration, start researching. Dig through design books and magazines and be unapologetic about bringing in pieces that will help make this place your perfect retreat.

SHORT ON SQUARE FOOTAGE

You can create spaces to serve more than one purpose. Start by determining the needs you have and how much space you have to work with. If you want to turn an extra room into a space for guests, but you also want it to work as an office when you don't have visitors, select furniture that will either serve or make room for both functions. For example, consider choosing a Murphy bed or a daybed that doesn't take up much space, so that you can also incorporate a desk or other furniture.

DON'T KNOW WHERE TO START

This type of space can be carved out in various shapes and sizes. So start small, with an area you can afford to lose. It can be as simple as the corner of a bedroom, the landing at the bottom of a stairwell, or a window seat. For example, you could turn a closet into a small craft area by setting up a narrow desk and adding shelving or lighting as needed. Small spaces are a great place to start reimagining creative ways to make every inch of your home useful for you.

BMC
Wash & Fold
· EST ·
— 1998 —

1121 SPEIGHT AVENUE
WACO, TEXAS

— Same Day Service —

Whirlpool cabrio

10

UTILITY ROOMS

Typically, when I am working with clients, they arrive at our first meeting with a stack of images they've been collecting for their one-day dream home. The majority of those photos are usually of kitchens and living rooms with some master bedrooms and baths thrown in for good measure. Very rarely do I see inspiration photos for mudrooms, laundry rooms, or pantries. When I try to dive into these rooms, my questions are typically met with blank stares: "I guess we just want our laundry room to look like a normal laundry room" is the usual answer. I think there must be some sort of misconception that not all rooms in our home can be created equal—that some get all of the thoughtfulness and attention to detail and the others just get what they get and we won't throw a fit. But for me, a home is not complete until every inch is serving its fullest potential. As weird as it may sound, it is often these utilitarian spaces that I stay up late into the night dreaming about. Many times, long after everyone else is asleep, I sit bent over my sketch pad imagining thoughtful ways to make the most hardworking rooms in a client's home not only exceedingly functional but also as beautiful and inspiring as the rest of the house.

I've labeled the spaces in this chapter "utilitarian" because they're typically confined to a pretty specific useful and practical function. These rooms are either intended to keep our families organized, help us prep for meals, or attempt to restrict the never-ending mountain of laundry to one small area of the house. These are usually among some of the most underestimated spaces and perhaps for a very good reason: They are not where we go to rest and gather and live life together with others. And I really get that mind-set, but I can't help but see this differently. If we were to consider the time that we spend doing these household tasks on any given day and over the course of a month or a year or a lifetime, we would see how the role of these rooms in those tasks is actually pretty important. So the efficiency with which we can operate due to the functionality of these areas starts to look like a wise investment. Intentional choices that create hardworking and beautiful spaces—places that we actually want to be in, that help make the work more of a joy—well, this is the kind of design work that excites me and makes it hard for me to sleep. For this reason, I tend to put a lot of thought and creative energy into these rooms because they have such a significant effect on how a family functions. If the design can affect your day that much or make tasks easier and create more time to spend with family, I want to make it a priority. So to me, these spaces serve an enormous purpose in a home.

In our own house, if my kids can't find me, they know there's a good chance I'm hanging out in the laundry room. While this may not commonly be someone's favorite room in their home, it has truly become one of mine. But it hasn't always been this way. When we moved into our farmhouse a few years back, I didn't have a laundry room at all. For the longest time I washed my family's clothes in a closet beneath the stairs, where there was enough space for only one overflowing hamper. As our children grew older, the pile of unwashed clothes grew higher each day, as did my mounting frustration in trying to operate from such a tiny space. I realized that even though the laundry wasn't going anywhere anytime soon, I could change the environment in which I did it. So I added some small, thoughtful details to that little closet wherever I could and made it a place I enjoyed being in even if I was knee-high in dirty clothes most days. I washed and folded from that closet for a long time, until eventually we decided that it would be a worthwhile investment to build out a larger laundry room. But for me, it hasn't been the extra square footage that makes me want to spend all day in there. It's the way I thought through the design of it and the things I included that now make it feel meaningful to me: potted plants, a few beloved antique vessels I use for storage, and some small art pieces that make me particularly happy. I also stocked up on my favorite scented candles just for this room. I made it into a place that feels like a retreat, with a table and chairs to sit and relax, and sure enough, it has totally reframed how I feel about this chore, which is no small thing.

I've said many times that the kitchen is the heart of a home. Well, I equally believe that the pantry is the heart of a kitchen. A lot of people might think that once that door is shut, who cares what's behind it? I've surely had this thought myself. But over the years, as I've spent countless hours in our own kitchen, I've learned that how my pantry functions in turn affects how well our kitchen runs—not to mention the effect it has on my own sense of joy as I prepare a number of meals each week. I now see that a few simple upgrades, like organizing ingredients in canisters I like or applying attractive labels onto shelves, can transform what could easily be a chaotic pantry into a helping hand, there to equip me with the tools I need for preparing meals. When I open my pantry and can easily grab the ingredients for a dish I'm making, the ease of finding them quickly feels like an encouraging whisper telling me: *You've got this*. And sometimes, that really does make all the difference.

If you're considering updating one of these areas in your own home, make sure you first establish the real needs of the space. Think through how it can work for you in the best possible way on a daily basis. The good news is it usually doesn't require a full redesign or renovation. It's not likely that you'll need to knock down any walls or buy all new furniture, unless, of course, you want to. It's usually the smaller details and that extra bit of effort to make it unique to you that allows any room to feel like a place you never want to leave.

Lots of people don't have a dedicated laundry room or mudroom. If that's the case for you, consider other spots in your home that could be creatively repurposed, like a portion of a hallway or a closet. Whether you are working with square footage to spare or just the corner of a room waiting to be rethought, the details that make this space matter are the same. They can be as simple as a functional feature, such as baskets on an open shelf above the washer. Or if the need is a larger folding area, you can easily add a countertop on top of your front-loading washer and dryer, and then put the same amount of thought into styling a small corner of it that you would put into a mantel or decorative shelf to make it feel finished out. It's amazing how adding a couple of pretty and practical items, thoughtfully arranged, can change the entire feel of a room. Opting for a bold, happy tile for the floor or walls can make a big statement. While this kind of element is often reserved for more common areas, the spaces in this chapter are where you could really use an extra dose of joy to get the job done.

My point is this: Just because these rooms are intended for a specific function doesn't mean they can't be beautiful and inspiring. The fun part is finding ways to infuse your personality into the design elements, transforming the rooms into places you actually enjoy spending time in. And for rooms where there is work to be done, I've learned that when you create a place that makes you happy, you won't mind spending time in it—no matter what its official function might be.

CRITICAL THINKING IN DESIGN

UTILITY ROOMS: WHAT TO CONSIDER

I've always enjoyed the challenge of creating inspiration in places where I need it the most. Hard-working spaces like the laundry room, pantry, and mudroom certainly top that list. But we spend a lot of time in these spaces, and because they really affect how our family functions and stays organized, I believe they're worth thinking through.

THOUGHTFUL ADDITIONS

- Notice how these homeowners have personalized their utilitarian spaces to be pretty, functional, and a true reflection of the people who use them.

FUNCTION AND ORDER

- Consider the organizational tools that are being utilized in these rooms and how they might improve the space you're working in.

THE ELEMENTS

- AMPLE STORAGE
- PRACTICAL SURFACES
- OPEN SHELVES
- UTILITY SINK
- HANGING ROD

- CUBBIES OR BINS
- PEG RAIL OR HOOKS
- BENCH OR WORK TABLE
- DRYING RACK
- ATTRACTIVE JARS AND CANISTERS

The owners of this home have successfully made rooms that are typically associated with chores and work, like this mudroom, feel inspiring. The mudroom boasts a unique blend of refined and raw aesthetics. The hardworking floors establish a sense of authenticity in the space while the trim and paint color add an emboldened traditional style. Functionality is emphasized with plenty of cabinet storage as well as with Shaker pegs for hanging jackets, coats, bags, and umbrellas. The art featured throughout this space helps elevate the mundane tasks of the day.

(*Left*) In this entryway, design details are encouraging functionality, such as the closed storage that hides away jackets and boots, as well as a bench that makes throwing your boots on easy as you head out. (*Above*) The homeowners have made the most of this nook that sits just off their kitchen by installing plenty of open shelving to store frequently used baking ingredients. They also turned the countertop space into a coffee bar, which helps to keep those everyday supplies off the counters in the primary kitchen area.

We packed a lot of character and charm into this butler's pantry by filling it with details that the clients love and wanted to enjoy even in a space this compact. The antique door and brick wall offer an old-world feel while the light gray cabinetry and brass hardware bring in a subtle traditional look. The checkerboard flooring and wood surface counter-top add more personality to the overall look, creating a nook that is truly tailored to the homeowners' style.

The ladder and glass cabinet doors bring efficiency and order to a laundry room that also doubles as an office. The stainless-steel elements used in this space reflect the industrial style that defines the rest of the house. If you're able to designate a portion of a room for laundry, consider using any leftover space for something altogether different—perhaps a work area—as these homeowners have done here, or dedicated to a craft or hobby. Sometimes a utilitarian space is the perfect location for a room to retreat to, despite how contradictory that may sound.

This mudroom shows that function and order don't have to be boring. The bold choice in paint color and the retro-inspired wallpaper elevate the entire look and purpose of the room. These same materials are mirrored in the family den, where I built out this desk from the single wall (*above*) to get the client a much-needed work area. The modern light fixture and chair make this space a comfortable and well-lit place to get things done.

Adding a sentimental piece to your kitchen, like these homeowners have with this re-
stored china cabinet, can make organization more enjoyable. Choose a piece with glass
doors if you want to show off what's behind them. A unique tile backsplash mixes new
with old, a characteristic of this couple's eclectic style, and is mirrored in the flooring of
the pantry and nearby mudroom (right) for a cohesive look. This built-in hall tree ties in
the wood and black details used in the mudroom and offers just enough storage space.
When space is minimal, an attractive pocket door is a great option.

Because this space is primarily used by the homeowner, she didn't hesitate to make it ultra fun and feminine. She chose to take what is typically a neutral room and make it playful and personal. The cabinet doors and hardware provide simple, modern lines so that the soft pink color is the real highlight of this laundry room. Balanced with the subtle design of the floor tile, the marble top and polished nickel of the island elevate this hardworking space while also referencing the more traditional style of the rest of the house.

When I'm designing a space for clients who have children, I try to cater my choices to fit the stage of life they're in. That was my goal with this multi-purpose room—that it be pretty and highly functional for this family of five. This room gets a lot of foot traffic because it's both the laundry room as well as the main place the family enters and exits the house. A handful of hooks on the wall and a few storage baskets are a good start toward maximizing space. You can install a countertop, like this one, that covers the washer and dryer to create a spot for folding. If space allows, cut out cubbies the size of large rolling laundry hampers to help contain the piles of clothing. Adding a hanging rod near the washer and dryer is another easy, practical update. I kept the stylistic elements true to the house's overall design style—updated traditional—which you see in the subway tile and fresh white cabinetry.

Space is well-utilized in the laundry room of this ranch home. Minimal square footage is maximized both practically, with sleek wood cabinetry and organizational baskets and canisters, as well as thoughtfully, with framed art prints that are significant to the family.

TROUBLESHOOTING

UNATTRACTIVE FUNCTIONAL PIECES

mudroom

- For a mudroom that's clean and tidy, install hooks behind cabinet doors for items that you'd like to keep hidden. You can also place baskets or build in drawers on a lower level of cabinetry for an easy place to toss shoes or other belongings. Upper cabinets can be used to store items that are not used every day. Incorporating attractive hardware can instantly transform the space.

laundry

- We spend a lot of time in our laundry room, so it should be as functional and as inspiring as possible. If you have the space, consider installing a cabinet desk where you can retreat to work or do something that you enjoy while the laundry is in cycle. If you're remodeling, adding open storage next to your washer and dryer to store a rolling laundry basket makes good use of space and allows you to hide dirty or laundered clothes while you're not using the space.

TIGHT ON SPACE

laundry room

- If you have a front-load washer and dryer, consider installing a counter on top of them to act as a folding space and additional surface. This is also a great spot to place baskets that conceal your laundry tools. You can also install cabinetry that reaches the ceiling, storing items on the top shelf that aren't everyday essentials.

pantry

- Consider utilizing small bins or clear, labeled jars to keep loose pantry goods organized. Small tiered shelves are great for storing canned goods and spices that need to be within reach.

FIREPLACES

Thank you for picking up this exclusive edition of Homebody. When I was conceptualizing this book, I knew I wanted to include an in-depth look at fireplaces, my favorite architectural feature in the home. They've always symbolized warmth and comfort to me, and whether you have a functioning fireplace or not, I hope you're inspired by these pages to create natural gathering places in your home.

Enjoy!

Joanna

BONUS
CHAPTER

OUR FARMHOUSE

When Chip and I decided to build out a master bedroom as an addition to our farmhouse, I wanted to ensure that it would blend with the home's original 1900s architecture. Fortunately, when we finished off the floor plan of the upstairs attic, we had flooring left over that was original to the house. That enabled us to repurpose the flooring in our bedroom, which makes this new construction feel like a natural extension. I also wanted to incorporate a working fireplace that would look and feel like the rest of the house, as the only prior fireplace in the house was non-functioning.

ARCHITECTURE

- ANTIQUED GLASS OVER MANTEL
- MANTEL LEDGE, HEADER, AND PILASTERS IN TRADITIONAL BLACK TRIM WORK
- CLASSIC BRICK FIREBOX
- WHITE BRICK HEARTH

STYLING

Our bedroom is styled primarily in muted tones, so I wanted this fireplace to be a bold addition. The floor-to-ceiling black trim creates a dramatic scene, allowing the antiqued mirrors to really stand out. The delicate brass candlesticks and vintage books add a layer of antique charm to the mantel.

THE REFRESHED CHATEAU

When Chip and I began flipping houses, we always ended up living in the homes we worked on. We were always looking at prospective properties, and without fail, I would gravitate toward the homes with fireplaces. In Texas, the time frame for actually using a fireplace is painfully short, yet having one began to feel like critical criteria to me. Because we were moving often, an unfamiliar house somehow felt more like home when it had a fireplace. Also, they are obvious architectural focal points, and I love dressing up a mantel with family photos and some pretty candlesticks. This fireplace is situated in one of the first houses Chip and I flipped in Waco. The ornate details weren't really my style, but I'd learned that it had been imported from Italy in the early 1900s and I loved the fact that it had so much history tied to it. This fireplace ended up being the only original architecture in the entire house that we left completely untouched.

ARCHITECTURE

- ORIGINAL ITALIAN REVIVAL SURROUND
- CRISP WHITE CROWN MOLDING AND COOL GRAY WALLS HELP CREATE A CLEAN AND REFINED LOOK, AND CONTRAST WITH THE AGED FIREPLACE MATERIALS
- SUBTLE MEDITERRANEAN-HUED TILE COLORS, FROM PEACH AND TERRA-COTTA TO LIGHT BLUES AND GRAYS

STYLING

I didn't want to remove any of the original character of this fireplace, so I curated the rest of the room's design around its style instead. I wanted it to feel like a piece of art itself, so I added pieces to the mantel that were simple and neutral in color. The architectural illustrations complement its color palette as well as nod to its European roots. Fresh branches cut from the yard bring a natural element to the mantel scape, while also creating movement against the squared-off edges of the photo frames and modern candelabra.

OUR FARMHOUSE

ARCHITECTURE

- ANTIQUE, NATURAL STONE FIREPLACE AND CHIMNEY
- PRIMITIVE SHELF MANTEL LEDGE
- BRICK-CLAD FIREBOX

STYLING

The rough-hewn stone structure really doesn't need anything else in order for it to stand out in this small space. I kept the styling minimal and practical with pieces that reflect how my family uses this garden shed.

THE ELEVATED RANCH

ARCHITECTURE

- GERMAN SMEAR STONE STRUCTURE AND CORBELS
- OVERSIZE ANTIQUE WOOD MANTEL LEDGE

STYLING

I softened the texture of this stone with artwork and greenery. Simple black-and-white frames and prints offer a modern counterpoint, while desert plants fit the raw aesthetic of this ranch home.

THE UPTOWN INDUSTRIAL

A fireplace seems to symbolize a feeling of home and warmth, no matter where it's located. While it may not be typical to place a fireplace in an entryway, this spot seemed like a great opportunity to make a statement right as you walk into this urban loft apartment. Its modern style and low-profile structure sets the tone for the rest of this industrial space.

ARCHITECTURE

- FLAT-WHITE STUCCO FIREPLACE SURROUND WITH MATTE BLACK CHIMNEY PIPE

- OAK WOOD SLAT WALL

- SLEEK ELECTRIC FIREPLACE

- BUILT-IN BENCH SEATING AND STORAGE HOOKS

STYLING

I had a local cabinetmaker install this white oak wall treatment to give the space some texture, which ended up pairing beautifully with the white stucco fireplace. I didn't want to overwhelm the minimalist design of this entryway, so I styled this fireplace with only a few large books and a couple of vases with simple silhouettes.

THE NOSTALGIC RETREAT

ARCHITECTURE

- ORIGINAL MANTEL WITH NEOCLASSICAL COLUMNS
- ANTIQUE MIRROR OVER MANTEL
- WHITE MARBLE SURROUND AND RAISED HEARTH
- BRASS TRIM AROUND FIREBOX

STYLING

I painted this original fireplace black for a bold, updated look. Delicate accent pieces, including vintage books and antique gold frames in different shapes and sizes, create a gathered look on the mantel.

THE LAYERED BUNGALOW

ARCHITECTURE

- REFINISHED MANTELPIECE
- CHARCOAL BLACK MARBLE SURROUND
- BROWN MILLWORK
- ANTIQUE GLASS PIANO HINGE TV CABINET

STYLING

A dark marble surround elevates the traditional style of this original fireplace. Antique glass bifold doors above the mantel soften the bold color of the accent wall and hide the television when it's not in use.

THE
HUMBLE ABODE

Before a remodel begins, I like to identify the focal point in the space and think through how I can draw that feature out in the final design. The original coffered ceilings in this living room almost serve as grid lines, drawing your eyes directly to the fireplace, so I really wanted to focus my attention on making this wall the highlight of the room. I emphasized the area by adding a marble surround to the fireplace and simple vertical wood paneling for subtle texture. By replacing the original built-in bookshelves that flanked both sides of the fireplace with windows, natural light now floods this space, once again drawing attention to the true centerpiece of the room: the fireplace.

ARCHITECTURE

- INSET FIREPLACE
- WINDOW SEATS
- VERTICAL WOOD SLAT OVER MANTEL
- TRADITIONAL TRIM WORK FOR MANTEL LEDGE AND SURROUND
- CARRARA MARBLE FIREPLACE SURROUND AND HEARTH

STYLING

I highlighted this mix of dimension, materials, and textures with clean-lined styling, as seen in the simple grouping of iron candlesticks and pair of classic black frames.

THE VINTAGE DWELLING

ARCHITECTURE

- BRIGHT WHITE STUCCO BUILD-OUT AND SURROUND
- BENCH-STYLE HEARTH
- SIMPLE WOOD MANTEL WITH BLACK METAL BRACKETS
- BLACK FIREBOX

STYLING

This simple wood ledge adds contrast to the large stucco build-out. A unique retro-style mirror mimics the size and impact of the fireplace while the brass bowl, colorful books, and potted plant add to the casual vibe of the overall space.

THE ECLECTIC FARMHOUSE

ARCHITECTURE

- MOROCCAN-INSPIRED TILE SURROUND
- THIN, WOOD MANTEL
- CONCRETE HEARTH
- BLACK FIREBOX
- PLASTER CHIMNEY

STYLING

The patterned cement tile makes a strong statement in this bedroom, so I layered the rest of the fireplace with organic elements, like white pottery and vintage books. A circular wood mirror acts as a simple counterbalance to the circular design found in the tile motif below.

THE SPACIOUS MODERN

ARCHITECTURE

- CONCRETE CLAD WALL
- ASYMMETRICAL WALL CUTOUT
- MODERN WOOD-BURNING FIREPLACE
- BRICK FIREBOX
- FLOATING HEARTH

STYLING

A floating concrete hearth and slanted cutout for stacked firewood makes a unique asymmetrical design statement. The exposed wood stack balances the cool tones of the fireplace and ties in the flooring and ceiling beams. Plants soften an otherwise unadorned space.

INDEX

ACKNOWLEDGMENTS

First, I'd like to thank the many families and individuals who have entrusted me with their homes over the last fifteen years. It has been a privilege to help you create spaces you love. And to all of the gracious homeowners and designers featured in this book, thank you for welcoming us into your home so that we could share your story with others.

This book is far more beautiful and valuable than I could have ever imagined. That is, in no small part, because of the creative talents and hard work of the following people:

To my home team at Magnolia: You not only help make dreams like this a reality, but you make every day along the way a whole lot of fun. To Emily Paben and Alissa Neely, thank you for being my first *and* last line of sight on this book, as well as with the countless other projects that come our way. To Kaila Luna, thank you for helping me put into words every story, lesson, and detail I wanted to communicate. To Hilary Walker, thank you for your sharp design eye and tireless enthusiasm to style (and restyle!) every shot to perfection. To Whitney Kaufhold, Cassie Robison, and Kelsie Monsen, thank you for leading the design and layout of this book. Your attention to detail never ceases to amaze me. To Kristen Bufton, Lindsey Hawkins, Laura Tucker, and the entire team at Magnolia Design and Construction, thank you for helping me create so many of the beautiful spaces featured in this book. And to the stylists, photographers, and assistants who helped along the way: Mackenzie Fulton, Becca Flannery, Ashley Maddox, Mike Davello, Beth Chiles, Kayli Nuce, and Hannah Harris.

To the photographers, Lisa Petrole and Cody Ulrich, thank you for capturing in stunning detail the story and personality of every home we featured. To Chris Hankins and Jay Hankins, thank you for your lovely illustrations. You all helped bring this book to life.

To David Vigliano, Bill Stankey, and Stephen Lewis, thank you for helping get this project off the ground.

To the team at Harper Design: Cristina Garces, Lynne Yeamans, Marta Schooler, Matt Baugher, Dori Carlson, and Stacey Fischkelta. Thank you for your around-the-clock support and expertise throughout this entire project.

To my family: It is and will always be my greatest honor to create a home for us to live life together. Thank you for being my inspiration. You are what home means to me.

HOMEBODY

the design template

Design affects the way we feel, whether we are conscious of it or not. It can impact our mood, our sense of well-being, and our desire to want to stay or leave a place. That's one of the reasons I am so passionate about design. I want to create places where people love to be and to show others that they are capable of doing the same. From the beginning of this book, I have encouraged you to look at photographs of rooms with a critical eye. Not for the sake of being critical, but rather to help you uncover your own personal style perspective. As difficult as it may have been to evaluate the spaces of strangers, it can be that much harder to look at your own home with fresh eyes. But you've stayed the course and you're ready. I believe in you.

First things first, go sit in the room that you want to tackle. It doesn't matter if you just want to make minor tweaks or take on a complete remodel. Observe the space for a few minutes and just take it all in. How does this room make you feel? How do you *wish* you felt in this space? Any thoughts here are really useful in charting the way forward and are worth jotting down in the notes section.

Here, I will lead you through how to use the fold-out design template at the back of the book, with sections designated for sketching, troubleshooting, and creating your own plan of action. This is the part of the journey where people can easily become overwhelmed or shelve the process for another time, but I encourage you not to put off making your home a place that you never want to leave.

Okay, let's get started!

SKETCHES

This first spot is for a basic floor plan of the room. I am a highly visual person and while I'm no artist, even a simple sketch can help me identify problem spots and places that need improvement. I like to lightly sketch out the room as it is now in pencil, and then layer on the updated floor plan in a different color as I make adjustments. You can start by taking stock of what you've got. Try to see all of the elements in this space from a new vantage point. Really inspect the furnishings, rug, light fixtures, windows, walls, hardware, art, and decorative pieces. Do this part slowly and thoughtfully. Is anything broken, outdated, dingy, or worn out? This is when you begin to determine what stays, what goes, and what just needs a little attention to make it work.

TROUBLESHOOT

02

Observe your space and write down any pain points that you can identify. Does the space feel cluttered? Do you have excess or inadequate furnishings in there? Does it feel cold to you? The fix could be as simple as adding in some warmer tones and textiles. Does it seem dark? Painting the walls a lighter shade, adding in additional lighting, or even enlarging windows to allow for more natural light to come in can make a huge impact in a space. Evaluate the color palette. Is it achieving the feel that you are going for? Do you have a rug and is it the right size for the room? Would the room benefit from adding any architectural details like trim or molding?

ELIMINATE

03

This is where it starts to get fun. Make a commitment to rid your home of the things you don't truly need or love. Consider what you can stand to lose and edit out any nonessentials. This will make room for you to really see the space. Sometimes clearing out a room has such a major impact that you don't need to do as much as you imagined. Editing out random stuff is the cheapest, easiest way to change the way a room feels. Again, if you don't really love an item and it isn't serving a valuable purpose, it's time to lose it.

INVEST

04

When you invest in something for your home it often requires time to save, plan, research, and acquire. I believe that this time spent is valuable and helps you to take ownership of each piece you bring into your home. You may need to be okay with some bare walls or incomplete furnishings, but I think those are small sacrifices on the way toward having a home that you love to be in. Begin by prioritizing your need and want lists. What pieces will make the biggest impact in your home? Which ones do you feel like you are most likely to love for the long haul? Rather than investing in trendy pieces that you may tire of quickly, consider classic or iconic styles that are much harder to lose interest in. Choose quality over quantity and trust your instincts.

MAKE A PLAN

05

Now it's time to figure out the actual action steps. What materials do you need to get the job done? Think through a color palette and specific pieces you want to add to the space. Are these DIY projects or do you need to bring in a professional? Take the time to plan rather than just jumping in without clarity on the direction you are headed. This will save you time and money and allow for you to mindfully gather the materials and elements you need on the front end. I'm in favor of doing the construction or remodeling portion of a room as quickly and efficiently as possible and then letting the decorating part evolve over time.

PRINT ADDITIONAL DESIGN TEMPLATES AT MAGNOLIA.COM/HOMEBODY

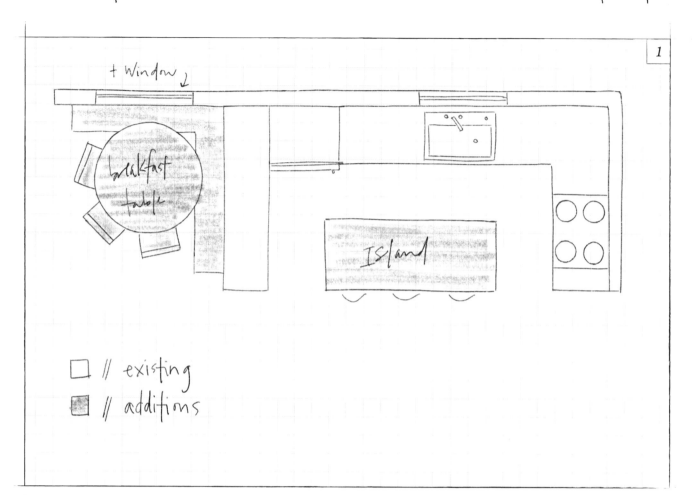

1

+ Window

breakfast table

Island

☐ // existing
⬛ // additions

Troubleshoot: **2**

- minimal countertop space
- no seating options
- outdated cabinetry
- poor lighting

Eliminate: **3**

- declutter counters
- remove upper cabinets to left of sink

Invest: **4**

- breakfast table
- comfortable chairs
- Island on wheels

Plan: **5**

- install bench seats around breakfast table
- add a window in breakfast nook
- add pendants above new island
- update cabinets w/ new paint + hardware
- add open shelving to left of sink

HOMEBODY

the design template

1

2

3

4

5